THE ENERGY WITHIN

THE ENERGY WITHIN

By Marie Cunningham MA

First published in Great Britain by Q-10 Publishing/Kildimo Books 2010

A catalogue record of this book is available from the British Library

ISBN 978-0-9566759-0-3

Q-10 Publishing, 11 Fallows Court, Middlesbrough, Teeside TF1 5LF
Website: www.theenergywithin.co.uk

Kildimo Books, PO Box 985, Canterbury CT4 5SB

Typeset in 12pt Perpetua by The Kildimo Partnership, Canterbury, Kent
Printed by Wealden Print, Hawkhurst, Kent

Dedication

To my wonderful children and grandchildren who are so special to me.
I thank them for their love and inspiration along the way.
I love you all dearly.

To my friends who have supported me through good and bad times.

I also dedicate it to anyone who has touched my life, past and present,
who brought in the experiences I needed to learn from.

Thank you to:
Everyone who believed in me, and all those who helped make this book
possible, especially Sarah Cheeseman BA for her editing and proofreading.

Contents

MARIE CUNNINGHAM

The Energy Within

THE GIFT OF KNOWING YOURSELF

www.theenergywithin.co.uk

CHAPTER 1

Letting Go

med to have everything. I had family, friends,
business.

something was missing in my life!

illed and the grip of this wasn't to let go of me

I listened to my language when serving in my

e students that attended my classes, the more I

e to live in the now; not to live for tomorrow, as

d will always be tomorrow.

py NOW – in the moment. I also taught them

eir homes and from their lives. But I had to ask

Vas I walking my talk? The issues that come with

important for me, as a childhood of hypocrisy

own life with a magnifying glass.

le I'd had a great longing to be in the sun, where

al pace of life existed. On previous holidays I sat

d tables, spending endless hours talking to each

iful sunsets, signifying the day was coming to a

ys I had the opportunity to start a business on the

but after spending months of happily arranging

mind at the last moment. My family had left after

waved goodbye, I closed the door and knew that

not happen if I lived in another part of the world.

in that old cookie, FEAR.

e and then, and decided not to go ahead and to put

time'. Years later, I'm realising the consequences

g in my life seemed to go right from that point.

Within months of changing my mind, our house set on fire. I went to work one morning, not knowing how my life was about to change.

The good news was that my daughter had stayed over at her boyfriend's and my son had left for work just after I had. But I didn't know that when I got the phone call from my friend to say that four fire engines were attempting to put out the blaze.

We lost practically everything, but the most painful part was losing our cat. He had been asleep in my bedroom when the fire happened and, needless to say, losing him broke our hearts. It took a few hours to get the raging flames under control, but watching them carry the cat from the house was the hardest part.

The firemen were so thoughtful and treated our feline friend with so much care. They even put an oxygen mask over his mouth to try to resuscitate him, but it was no use; the smoke had been so thick and black. It was only after the third run into the house that they found him huddled under my duvet.

Everyone kept telling me I should be grateful it wasn't a child and I was, but it didn't take away the pain of losing him, as he was part of our family. I also found it strange that many people around me couldn't allow me to grieve the situation. It was a case of I should be thankful for what was safe, rather than be grieving for what I'd lost.

I knew that if I could have had all my possessions back or the cat, then I would have chosen the cat. This might sound like an easy choice to make, but I had no house insurance and had to start from scratch to get the things we needed. Friends and neighbours were amazing, taking us in until we found somewhere to rent, and they even had a collection for our basic needs, such as towels, etc. We had to move into a rented house for six months while the top floor and attic of our home were being rebuilt.

Many times after the fire I would go to look for something and search frantically, actually forgetting for a moment that the fire had happened. Then it would hit me that the item had probably melted in the heat; after all, if a television could melt away, what chance would something as fragile as a photo have?

At first, when I realised my first-born's shoe and beautiful blonde curl of his hair were gone forever, my heart ached.

But we store things up in the attic to visit the memories, to remind us of happy times, yet really those memories are in our hearts, so they're going nowhere. I started asking the questions, why do we hold on to so much? Why do we keep things for so long? Why do we need to remind ourselves of the past?

I knew a little about the subject of Feng Shui and this helped me to understand a little about energy in general. I realised that everything in our life is symbolic of the self. I picked up my folder and began reading this ancient wisdom. It told me that the house represents the self, and the loft represents our mind, where we store away so many things to remind us of happy times.

However, in our subconscious we bury information of sad events, etc., and just like the attic, now and again we need to clear it out. But clearing out is hard for many people, as it's like losing a part of the self. I know when I stayed with a friend recently and suggested it would be good for her to have a clearout, she nearly had a nervous breakdown at the thought of it.

I also learnt that fire is symbolic of anger that's stored, and eventually, like all energy, it has to explode (as energy expands). It's a little like a volcano, or a pressure cooker: when too much pressure builds up it has to be released, and humans are just the same. All of our trapped emotion (energy) has to go somewhere, and when it isn't allowed to be released in a healthy way, it stagnates in the body.

'The significant problems we have cannot be solved at the same level of thinking with which we created them.' – Albert Einstein, Theoretical Physicist

I'd been reading *Living Magically* by Gill Edwards on a regular basis and would often come across the term 'we create our own reality'. I fought myself for a long time; after all, why would I bring such a horrific event into our lives? As I lay in a strange bed in another part of town, away from my friends of twenty years, I'd go over it in my head as to whether it was my 'fault'.

Remembering the experience of watching my life go up in smoke, and holding on to my daughter as we heard the creaking windows expand with the pressure of the heat, the last thing I needed to believe was that I'd brought it into our life.

It took me a long time to get my head around why the fire happened.

As with a lot of things in life, it's only after the event that we can look back with a certain level of detachment and see the bigger picture.

Could I really have created it in some way?

On what level would I have wanted to do this?

I suppose in all honesty I loved my home. I had my friends nearby and many good memories there, but I also had many bad memories of the house. A lot of pain, hurt and anger were stored in that house, including that hardcore, gut-wrenching pain of relationships breaking. So, if I am honest, I'm not surprised it eventually exploded, with all the emotions of twenty years crammed into the building.

What I found extremely difficult was the fact that I was doing an Angel workshop when the fire started, and I cried to God as to why they couldn't show me a sign so that I could go home and at least save the cat. After all, I had had many insights for other people in the past, so why not for myself on this occasion?

I had to realise there was a higher purpose.

It has certainly been a learning curve for me, especially in terms of how to be honest with my feelings, as I would always try to keep the other person happy rather than myself. I now know that was not the best or healthiest way to live. Mind you, I have lost a few friendships since I started to be true to myself!

Thankfully, most people sort out and vent their feelings in a healthy way, but there are many who are not in a position to do so; those who rarely let their true feelings show and, if not careful, could end up with problems such as arthritis, cancer, etc., as these are usually signs that a person is holding on to energy, especially anger.

Illness is one of the main reasons people get into 'new age' thinking, or it could be due to heartache, bereavement or a crisis in general. Then the questions start: What's life all about? Why are we here? Where are we going? and so on. Then we want answers, and quickly. It's not enough that someone points us to the right book; we want them to read it and explain it to us.

We often don't want to put in the hard work of finding out how IT, the universe, works. I don't mean the solar system, I mean our own universe, our central point of being. By *central point of being* I mean our head office, or our higher self.

My soul is the central point; it resides within the temple (ME).

Just as I, the physical body, reside within my home, which resides within its village or estate, which resides within a town, country and so on.

Therefore, I am the centre of MY universe. I create what is going on around me; how can I not? If I am energy first and physical after, then it all has to start with me!

I now believe that if we sort out what's on the inside, we'll understand what's happening on the outside. I'd started reading books on metaphysics, crystals, etc. around seven years before the fire, so I had a little knowledge on the subject, although many times I'd put down the book and not have a clue what I'd just read because I just didn't understand the language in many of them.

I found that many of the books I read just made me feel stupid; many of the words were alien to me. I remember hearing the word metaphysics many times in a class I was attending, and it took me until about the fourth class to get up the courage to ask what it meant!

'Anything outside the physical,' my teacher said; meta = beyond.

Gill Edwards' *Living Magically* was a godsend to me, as I understood her language and she didn't make me feel that the *crap* in my life was my 'fault'. She taught me, however, that it was my responsibility, that I'd created it, not as some form of punishment from God, but as an experience that my soul could learn from.

This was a huge statement for a woman who thought life just didn't like her. I'd come to believe that the saying 'The harder your life is, the closer to God you'll be' meant that I'd one day be sat on his knee. I must admit, I threw her book away three times before finally reading it properly. I just didn't want to hear her language. How could I create all the pain and hurt I'd had in my life (and there was a lot) and, plain and simple, why would I want to?

I've come a long way since reading that book and I must take my hat off to the author's outstanding work; I'd like to think I might meet her one day, just to say thanks for helping me to get my life in order.

A couple of years before I started looking at metaphysics I came across the subject of chakras and was curious as to what it was all about. I looked at the poster for a long time before putting the book back on the shelf, as I didn't understand what chakras were. They had different colours, which all had a meaning, and a Sanskrit name, etc.

I decided they were too complicated for me and left the shop.
I'd do the same with crystals, as although I liked them I didn't understand what their properties were. I kept thinking I was not clever enough, as I'd

never even sat an exam at school! That's how the idea for this book came about. Customers in my shop, The Crystal Cave, started mentioning the fact that I spoke in 'normal' language, making this subject easy for them to understand.

The seed was planted for a book that speaks to the average person on the street; the person who may not know where to start with this fascinating subject. The aim of this book is to help those who want to step into the world of ENERGY.

I'd like people to understand that to be a healer, or a psychic, you don't have to be born a 'seventh son of a seventh son' or into any special family group, or to have lived in an ashram for years. We are all healers. *Anyone who can love can heal*.

We all have a sixth sense, we're just not educated on how to use it. You've probably had the experience of knowing when the phone's about to ring, or when someone is ill. That's using your sixth sense.

Over time, I noticed I was changing. My tastes began to change, such as the music I listened to, as did my attitude towards everything around me. My world started to take on a different view. What I didn't know was that I was getting ready to *switch on*, or *wake up* as it's known by some people.

There are many terminologies for this: walking the path, finding the self, to name a few, but it simply means learning how to be aware of the self. It doesn't mean being all love and light, or being some fluffy bunny. This would not serve us, as we are made up of positive and negative energy (like the yin/yang symbol). A lack or too much of either will put us out of balance.

To achieve balance is our duty.

The basic intention in life is to be truly happy, and balance will achieve this.

Our responsibility to our self is to learn how to read beyond what we see physically and to understand the messages being given and received daily. Once we do this, our lives become so much easier, happier and joy-full.

When we become disillusioned or powerless in a situation, we've usually taken our attention to the past and we look at who/what we lost, or we look to the future to a time when things will be different (better). Yet, if we could stay centred in that moment and experience the FULL experience and FEEL the feelings, we would empower ourselves.

Being in the moment isn't easy in today's climate, as we are bombarded with products that won't allow us this luxury. We are encouraged to buy Easter eggs in January or Christmas cards in September. But all we have is the moment! The words you have just read in the last line have gone and the pages to come have not yet arrived; all you have is the moment you are in now.

Being centred and in the moment is to be self-empowered, meaning not giving our energy to anyone/anything else. Try to remember that any discomfort you are feeling at any particular moment in your life is trying to show you something. I now think the term healing, or letting go, is a little misunderstood, as any experience we've had is part of us and has made us who we are.

The fire in our home taught me a great deal about myself and my life in general. The most important thing it taught me was how to unload the useless emotions I'd carried for so long.

But this didn't happen overnight and certainly not with ease, as the past few years have been *event-full* to say the least and I am sure I could write another book on what's happened.

I needed reminding that the most important things in my life are my family and true friends, as they will always be there for me. I learnt that love is the only thing that's real and that our health is of vital importance.

To make the change I needed, I had to start with being honest, not only with others, but also with myself. This isn't always easy, as we are brought up to be polite more than honest, especially in the English culture. Often, fear takes over, as we're frightened that if we offend the other party we may hurt or lose them.

> *'In your life's defining moments there are two choices, you either step forward in faith and power, or you step backward into fear.'* —
> James Arthur Ray, Creator of Harmonic Wealth®

So, more often than not, we swallow our true point of view to keep the other person happy, and in the process we make ourselves unhappy. We literally *swallow our words*, often causing ourselves throat/neck problems.

After the fire, without realising it, I started to put all my energy into my business, making it my life, even to the point where it came before my family commitments. I no longer had time for anything; I was too busy! This way I could avoid my true feelings. It meant I had no time to look at why my back ached or why I had a cold, and I didn't realise what an effect it was having on me, or those around me.

I didn't want to show my feelings of pain and anger or all the other emotions that were swirling around inside. After all, I'd lived in that house for more than twenty-five years. I'd brought up my children there and, after having a childhood of moving from room to room and bedsit to bedsit with my mother, my home had become my castle.

After six months our home was put back together, but when it was time to move back in, it didn't feel like MY home any more. Nothing felt right and the memories of that day wouldn't go away. My daughter continued living with her boyfriend and eventually, my youngest child left home. I was left alone with nothing but my memories. I now understand that certain events in life are here to get us to turn a corner and this had been one of them – what I now call a realisation moment.

While all of this was going on, I still had the feeling I wanted to live abroad.

But I also still had the fear of leaving. What if they all forgot me?

I just didn't have the courage it took to completely let go.

After a lot of soul searching, I eventually told myself I was ready to sell the house and go. But after selling, I hung around for another eighteen months, living with friends and family, and even sleeping over at the shop. This became very unhealthy for me, not to mention my family and friends, as I was uncovering parts of me even they didn't like.

I'd be moody and dependent, causing me to look at many issues in my life.

I was like a cripple who had dropped her crutches, unstable and afraid of falling.

I was the frightened little child again.

I knew I had to start searching for who I really was, as I'd started having many problems with my feet and legs, which I knew represented moving forward in life or staying stuck in the past.

I knew I had to do something.

I KNEW what I taught was the truth.

So I looked at my life and my body, and asked my soul what it wanted.

I decided I had to let go of everything and see if this walking my talk would work.

I sold my car...

How much could I trust this energy system called the universe?

I then got the courage to sell the shop and I finally let go...

Chapter 2

Full Circle

I TRAVELLED to the many places I'd always wanted to see, including Southern England to visit the ancient site of Stonehenge. It was breathtaking to stand alongside those huge stones and I could feel my forehead buzzing as I walked around them.

I then went on to Greece for a few weeks to see if I still felt the same about the islands, and I did. Next, I went to Italy, as I'd just finished reading Dan Brown's *Angels and Demons* and I wanted to trace the maps from the book. I felt like I was on a real-life adventure and I realised that this was in fact the very first time in my life that I'd experienced total freedom.

For the first time I actually owed no one anything, as I'd paid off all my debts and didn't have a rota to stick to. Each day I could decide if I wanted to stay where I was or move somewhere else. I had no one to answer to. It was all very new to me and, at times, felt very alien.

Then I went on to India, where I lived in a village for a while and had the chance to experience real life there. I had many great experiences and met some wonderful friends who taught me that life should be simple. I saw how people can live without huge flat-screen TVs and computers, and that *family time* together is high on their list of priorities.

My next call was Australia, when I decided to surprise my cousin and her family. Although I was happy while I was in these beautiful places, I found that I still had to keep coming back home, as I missed my family and friends, especially my grandchildren. But when I was back in my hometown, I felt I didn't belong there either and would put pressure on everyone to be with me. When I didn't get the attention I wanted (remember, attention = energy), I interpreted it to mean that they didn't love me.

What pressure to put on those I loved!

I knew better than that!

Deep down I knew I wasn't alone; we are never alone!

That statement can be hard to swallow, as many people do not know that we have a guiding force. But I know it's true that we are never truly alone in life. It just seems that way to us when we feel low, or afraid.

I'd previously learnt that my back represented support, and although I knew the pain in my back was due to a severe injury I had suffered in a car crash, I was starting to realise that when the problem with my back reoccurred it was because I wasn't accepting the support the universe was sending me, as I was out of balance, which meant I was closed off.

And all the time I'd been thinking it represented my family not supporting me...

I was simply reading it wrong!

Could that have been why I'd had problems with my throat and ears?

Could I not be getting the message?

When we learn to read the signs we are given daily, life gets easier. It's when we don't trust ourselves that things become difficult for us. But learning to read the signs isn't always easy, as our attention is often on something/someone else because we aren't taught to believe that we know what is best for us. We're told to trust the government, church leaders, doctors or in fact anyone on TV that can tell us how to have a better life by selling us a quick fix, and we distract ourselves in any way we can from what we could be looking at.

It happened to me recently in India. It was 6 a.m. and I had bumped into a friend on the shoreline, as we'd both decided to catch the sunrise. As we walked and chatted I spotted an unusual-looking red crab walking along, and I kept trying to catch Dan's attention to show him. I didn't know that he was smiling as he watched my behaviour, as I was getting rather frantic because he wasn't looking at what I was pointing out.

Eventually, I looked at him and he calmly nodded to what he had been looking at: around twenty red crabs walking along in the opposite direction. I started to laugh as I watched them and said to Dan that this was very symbolic of my life! I was so busy looking at one thing, I was missing the bigger picture. *Another realisation moment!*

Due to the fact that this subject isn't taught as part of our natural teachings, we fear it, and fear plays such a huge part in our lives because it holds us back. And it's not just fear of failure that stops us, but also fear of success. But by being controlled by such things as fear, etc. we create a frequency that feeds the fear vibration and so on.

Fear is a low vibration and love is a high one.

People often come to me asking for help with spirits in their home. I explain that a spirit is not always the cause, as often our mind creates the worst possible scenario. We pick up on energy every day, often without realising we are doing it. Just think of a time when you've walked into a house where there's been an argument and you felt that you could cut the atmosphere with a knife.

The energy of the argument, unless defused properly, will stay around, often drifting off to a corner of the room. Sometimes at night, when the energy of the house is calmer as everyone is asleep, this energy may start moving and bump into something, causing a noise. As energy doesn't die, it only transforms itself and, as like attracts like, a bad mood or argument will give off a low vibration, attracting a similar energy.

Today, there are many examples of how metaphysics works.

We need to watch our thoughts and fears, as what we fear most comes to us. In the film *Never Ending Story*, the boy faces the swamp of sadness and the 'Mirror of himself'. These examples are a good way to help us understand how we must face ourselves.

The Matrix is another good film showing how to receive messages from the think tank. Remember the part where he's told 'life is not real' and eventually, realises that he is 'the one'. I believe we are all 'the one', as we are all made from the God-force (source) that created us.

Sadly, not trusting the self and believing what others say instead of our self is how many people live their lives. Why is this? It's how we've been programmed. It's very important for us to remember who we really are under all the layers of protection we've applied, all the guises we've created, so that no one gets to know the real us.

Let's face it; many of us haven't a clue who we really are!

'Out of all the wonders in the world, the most incredible thing in your whole life is already inside you.' — Richard Wilkins, The Yellow Book

We must stop living the life we think we should have and live the one we want. Therefore, it has to start with the *self*; it cannot start anywhere else. Once we accept who we really are, warts and all, and stop judging ourselves, we will have inner peace and inner love.

CHAPTER 3

A Loving Creation

FOR YOU TO BE HERE in this life at this moment, all the stars in the galaxy had to be of the right vibration; not a fraction more, or less, for life on the planet to be created in the first place. *That in itself is a true miracle.*

Then, the two people who were to become your parents had to be in the right place at the right time to meet. Then, when the time was right, the sperm and the egg had to be the correct ones to make YOU the *special* human being that you are. At the time of those two forces of energy joining together, no one could imagine the life YOU would create. That's right! The life you created for yourself. All the people you would meet and all the events that came about just because YOU are in the world.

Yes, people's lives that have been changed, just because they met YOU!

I realise that this could be a hard concept for those who are still hurting in some way, or who might be feeling low and might not feel they have touched people's lives. But every person you walk past, or speak to, will be affected by this contact. What a concept to take onboard, and difficult for some people to believe, especially those with no self-worth.

But that's why the journey of self-discovery is worth it, as when we find ourselves, we literally become beacons of light. Then, others will be attracted to the light, like moths to a flame. Do you realise this could mean that all you need to do to help those you love to heal is simply to heal *yourself*?

Can it be that simple?

Can we really be that important to the universe?

I think so (now), but it's taken me a long time to really believe it, and although hard to achieve at times, it was worth it to see the transformation taking place within.

But transformation of any kind can be a struggle. Just think of the caterpillar changing into a butterfly and the fable of a boy who was watching the struggle. As the butterfly was trying to get out of its cocoon, he thought he would help it along and broke away some of the cocoon, only to find that when the butterfly came out, his wings were deformed and he couldn't fly. Struggling is nature's way of strengthening.

Thankfully (and I only say thankfully on a day when I'm in a healthy state of mind), my children are wise enough to know that when I'm going through struggle they can't help and they literally leave me to it. They know that if they try to fix it for me, it will not serve me.

Although when I'm in the state of 'victim' I moan that they don't care for me, etc. etc., once I'm over it, I'm thankful they allowed me to learn my experiences in the way I needed to. If they interfered, their actions would have an effect on the outcome, as we are all connected to each other and each act will affect another life force on this planet.

Think about it this way; if we breathe in the air that someone else has just breathed out, how can we not be connected? That same energy has been part of plants, animals or other humans. We pull the energy (energy = information) from the system (system = the universe) and then in turn give it out to other life systems and have an effect on them.

Stop for a moment and think about this concept.

We attract events to us so that we will learn and grow.

The energy is brought in and then used how and when we need to use it. As it's affected by the mood or vibration we are in at that moment, we then return it back into the world. All of this is going on and we don't even know we are doing it.

How can we deny that we are not all interconnected?

Surely, it's our birthright to be taught this from childhood, as we really haven't got a clue how powerful we are. The question is, what are you doing with your energy? What are you sending out into the world?

> '*What this power is I cannot say; all I know is that it exists and it becomes available only when a man is in that state of mind in which he knows exactly what he wants and is fully determined not to quit until he finds it.*' – Alexander Graham Bell, Scientist and Inventor

I suppose one of the questions to start is: do you love yourself? Does that question make you cringe? That one was the biggie for me, too. I actually thought I was okay with myself, as I'd read many books on self-help, worked with crystals for a while and had many therapies. But at a workshop one day, I was asked to hold a mirror and say to my reflection, 'I love you'. I just couldn't do it and the thought of it actually made me feel sick at the time.

Should be simple, shouldn't it?

Can you? Find a mirror and have a go! The reason this is a hard exercise for many people is because of the programming we've had from birth. We are told not to be vain, not to love ourselves, not to put ourselves first. But if we don't, how can we look after anyone else?

I witnessed this firsthand many years ago when I was bringing up my children as a one-parent family. I'd woken up one morning and couldn't move to get out of bed. I actually thought I'd had a stroke. The doctor was called to the house and, after examining me, he told me I was suffering from something called 'burnout' because I was doing too much and that I had to stop, before it was too late. He said I needed to drop some of the balls I was juggling or I'd burn out altogether. My body was certainly reflecting this.

I was trying to take care of the children, I was working and was also trying to take care of my elderly mum as well as another relative. My friend Lorraine sat me down and explained that I was like a spinning top with so many people relying on me, and just like a spinning top, I had to spin at the correct speed to stay in balance.

As I was doing everything for everyone but me, and I'd run out of steam (steam = energy). If the speed (energy) of the spinning top isn't correct, then the top slows down and eventually falls over, and anything that's around it falls over too.

This is such an important statement!

If we don't keep our own energy high, how can we be strong enough to help another? Therapists are often the worst culprits for this, as most of their time is spent doing treatments for others and they never get around to receiving what they need themselves. I am not saying this is true of all therapists, but a large number I've met fall into this category, myself included many times.

So, if information (energy) is beamed to us on a daily basis (although I believe it is more so generated within us), all we have to do is learn to read this energy and to listen to our bodies. I know I talk a lot about energy, but everything IS energy. It can't be anything else really.

If we feel something, it's energy.

If we think something, it's energy.

If we desire something, it's energy.

Down to the tiniest point within ourselves are the atoms that make us what and who we are, energy, and if you close your eyes a little and look at the window, you can actually see these little black and white holes of energy.

Our body is a protein-producing machine. The brain, heart, skin, etc. are all systems in our body working individually, and for each part to work to its full potential all parts need to work together, as the neurons that connect to each other form a sort of 'net'. As we build our memory bank on what we believe life to be (through our experiences), we make that 'net of information' stronger, which carries on creating our 'identity'.

The moment we experience a certain emotion, such as anger or love, the hypothalamus will assemble peptides, which enter different parts of the body and connect to a thing called the receptor, which sends signals to the cells.

The energy we are made up of is both masculine and feminine (not to be confused with male and female) and even the formation of the atom is due to the clustering of negative electrons around a positive one. This unification starts the creative process, as the feminine particles vibrate rapidly under the influence of the masculine energy and circles around it. The result is the birth of a new atom.

> 'As is the human body so is the Cosmic body. As is the human mind so is the Cosmic mind. As is the microcosm so is the Macrocosm. And as is the atom so is the Universe.' – The Upanishads Spiritual Hindu Scriptures

Even our thoughts are generated this way, as when we have an idea it goes into the ether like a hologram and is then either manifested by us when the conditions are right or it's picked up from the ether and lodged in the mind of another person.

The problem is, as the thought grows and develops, it's eventually regarded as belonging to the person who picked it up. Often, we have a great idea but do nothing with it; then we hear someone has created what we'd only thought about. This will become more and more common as we go into the next stage of evolution, as we are becoming more intuitive and telepathic.

Strong people use their mental will to produce and implant their thoughts into the minds of the masses, causing them to think in a certain way. As people who are easily led tend not to have thoughts and ideas of their own, they are easy to influence. Movies are a great example of this, in terms of how they make us angry, scared or upset, etc.

Do you realise the brain processes 400 billion pieces of information per second, yet we are only aware of 2,000 of them. We haven't a clue how powerful we are, as we only use a small part of what we have available to us. However, things are rapidly changing and people want to know how we can change the way we think.

In 1993 an experiment was carried out in Washington DC with around 4,000 volunteers from different countries, where they meditated on peace for long periods and actually saw a 25% drop in violent crime. Surely this tells us something?

Always remember that energy doesn't die, it only transforms. A love energy (feeling) can quickly turn to hate, or a bad mood can soon turn to a good one.

Everything has an order and I believe we call this order GOD.

I once heard Deepak Chopra explain what he believed God stood for, and it certainly made sense to me.

G – Generation

O – Organisation

D – Deliverance

Everything goes through this process, including a thought, as it's generated and then goes through some kind of process of organisation before it's delivered. Take this book! It had to start with a thought from the person who suggested it to me before it became manifested in the physical world.

And as everything starts with a thought, it's important to watch them!

If we master that one then I think we've cracked it; although it seems to be one of the hardest things to achieve, as our thoughts tend to rule us in many ways as they float around in a sea of energy, all interacting and evolving.

Thoughts are so powerful (full of power), and a thought holds only a *slight* vibration unless it carries an *emotional* connection, when it gets much stronger. Remember a time you were having a bad day? The day might not have started too well – you may have had slept badly or had bad dreams (be careful not to get drawn into the memory when doing this, though) – and you try to shake it off, but it doesn't leave completely.

You may go out for a bit of retail therapy, but what happens then? You go into a thicker soup of energy in the shopping area and, as like attracts like, we have everyone else's emotions (e-motion = energy in motion) running amok too.

Or maybe you can recall being in a really good mood, you're getting on with your housework and you may decide to sit down and have a coffee break. So you pick up a magazine and read about someone who's been hurt or deceived by a loved one. You read how he/she broke the other's heart and suddenly, you are back in time and feeling old emotions. What's just happened?

Your thought has hooked itself to an emotion that you've held on to and which has been lying dormant in your system. So you could end up feeling the same pain that an ex-partner caused you many years ago. Your mood has gone from peace to anger and you haven't even left the sofa.

If you imagine a sea of energy floating around you and you realise that like attracts like, you can begin to get a picture of how it all works. So it makes sense to keep our energy healthy by watching our thoughts so that we can attract healthy situations in our life.

Our body is always trying to keep us happy and it will create its form from how we have been thinking, as the physical body is usually about a week behind the subtle bodies. The secret is to stay centred and balanced and live in the moment, in the NOW, as that way we'll make choices from a healthier point of view.

'*We see the world not as it is, but as we are.*' – Ken Keyes, Personal Growth Leader and Peace Advocate

Think about that one. What does it mean?

Some people call it mirroring. The vibration we send out from our energy field is what the universe 'sees' and it gives us more of the same, as like attracts like. Therefore, we attract more of what we think. So always remember the basics!

Everything is ENERGY – a vibration, a colour.

We are literally a rainbow of vibration, as a human energy field is made up of thoughts, beliefs, fears and emotions from the programming we receive from birth of who we are. Every thought, word or emotion we are given will change our energy field in some shape or form. Even what we take in through TV, newspapers, etc. will change our vibrational field.

Our energy field (aura) helps us function in the world by providing us with information *energetically* through our *thoughts and emotions*. But if our intention of what we want is based on fear, then that's what we give out to the world, and likewise, if based on love.

Let's take the example of being in love. We see the best of someone when we are *aligned* with this frequency, freeing up our *controlling* energy. This could also be what is referred to as the rose-coloured glasses stage, as we see things through a pink haze, as the energy of love that we send from the heart chakra is pink.

When we get to the stage of using our ego in the relationship, which is a more controlling energy, we work with the solar plexus chakra, using yellow energy and a different frequency. Things often start to go wrong with relationships when people are working from the solar plexus, as it's about using personal power and will (willpower).

If we realise that a thought comes first and an experience comes second, then we could take on a healthier slant with our lives, as our experience is always a reflection of what we're thinking.

Our brain acts like a large antenna picking up energy and information, as anyone who has been peaceful before going into a large town or city may have experienced a change of mood on returning home.

Of course, we must be responsible for our thoughts, but most importantly we must be aware of them. For instance, the thought of not being good enough or not being lovable, etc. will attract people into our life that reflect this to us. Or, thinking 'no one loves me' will result in having no one around, as that energy sent out from our system will actually repel people and they will not want to come in.

Being *aware* of what kind of thoughts we have is very important.

A friend gave me a good technique to discipline our thoughts if we're going through a negative stage and being hard on ourselves. Put an elastic band on your wrist, and each time you say or think something negative about yourself snap it on your wrist. It works a little like tapping a dog on the nose. It's surprising how quickly we stop our negative thoughts with this technique. It also helps us to become aware of how we're thinking.

Holding on to feelings of hurt, *resentment*, etc. is a major problem for many people, as they find it hard to let them go. But holding on to them isn't healthy either; it's healthier to let go and allow our energy to flow freely, creating a *flowing* life force of energy, as when we hold on to something for a long time we create a contraction in our system (our aura).

This can be a feeling, thought, idea, belief or a need in the emotions. In fact, anything we are holding on to is a waste of our energy. Instead of using it to create what we are aiming for, we waste it by holding on to old feelings and ideas that really serve us no purpose.

It's very important that our intention in what we desire is crystal clear each day and we must begin by being honest with ourselves. Although difficult at times, it's achievable with enough discipline. We must learn to trust that whatever's happening is in our best interests and realise that there's always a payoff for whatever situation we're in.

> '*The physical manifestation of a disease is a phantom. It's the cell's memory that is addicted; memory is more important than matter.*'
> – Deepak Chopra MD

Payoff was another term I had trouble understanding when I first heard it. Some people call a payoff 'a lesson', although I don't like using the word lesson, as for some people it may bring up a childhood memory of 'I'll teach you a lesson'. A payoff is simply a swap of energy (getting something in return for something given).

A few years ago I was in a situation where I was constantly moaning about having to visit an aunt in hospital when my life was so busy. In class my friend Alex said the words that would bring up a lot of anger. He asked why I was putting up with the situation instead of letting it go. I told him I couldn't let go and he asked me what my 'payoff' was.

I'd never heard this term before and resented him even thinking I was doing it for a payoff of some kind. I asked:

'Why must I be getting a payoff?'

I'd also started defending myself and told him I was putting up with the situation out of love for my aunt (but at the time, she was really pushing my buttons). After a long, drawn-out and heated discussion, I went away quietly to make coffee for the group, with the word 'payoff' dancing around in my head.

In the discussion he'd had the cheek to say:

'Even what you do for your children has a payoff.'

I really retaliated to that one. I'd told him he didn't have a clue what he was talking about. After all, we do what we do for our children without wanting anything in return, or do we? While making the coffee I could hear his words in my head.

'What happens when you dress your children and they look great?'

'People comment on how well they look, or how well they behave, or how you've done a good job, they are a credit to you.'

Then, it was like a light bulb going on in my head.

I had to be honest with myself and realise that I did indeed have a payoff with my aunt: that if I didn't look after her I wouldn't get the praise she always gave when telling others how 'she didn't know what she'd do without me'.

In all honesty, I was resenting all the running around, and even deeper than that, I actually *didn't* want to look after her, as I was carrying very deep resentments and pain from my childhood. The bottom line, and the root of my problem, was *resentment* at having to be there for her, when deep down inside I felt that she hadn't been there for me when I needed her as a child.

Those resentments were still inside my system after all those years, and I didn't know it until this discussion.

I went back into the room and told him that I finally understood what he meant, which opened up a very interesting discussion with the group, as many of them were like me and didn't like what he'd said. From then on I started looking at everything in my life and he was right, we do get payoffs all the time; although many are more comfortable with the term 'payback', as *everything* we do will give us some kind of return!

Admitting to payoffs is a difficult task, but a very useful one once we start being *truly* honest with ourselves, as our thoughts/memories are like files in a filing system: we put them away and forget about them. Think of your mind as a computer; we put information on it, work with it and then close it down. The next time we turn it on, we see what we've put on the system, as it's there until we decide we no longer need it and erase it.

How many of us decide to save it and often make a back-up disc?

We often overload our system with information that has no relevance to our lives in the present time. How many files and old programs do you have clogging up your system? You can tell a lot about yourself by your computer!

We have a great system inside, a part of us that knows our answers. Inside, we have a *wizard* (if you don't feel right with the word wizard, use the word guide) that has the answers we need. We're actually born to discover our inner wizard/guide and we can learn to hear its voice, which usually speaks in the silence known as meditation. It's in the silence that we create what we want and this is why meditating is so important, as it means getting in contact with our *core self*.

Sit and look all around you, and identify the furthest thing you can see; realise that every point in the cosmos is your central point. When we stop our inner turmoil, we realise that we are the centre of our own universe; therefore, we create what is happening in *our world*. Each of us has experiences that no one else can experience.

Our inner guidance knows the secrets of immortality: that we never die and therefore there was never a time when we didn't exist in some form or other. If you can't get to grips with what's said here, just think of gold. It doesn't matter what form it takes — gold can be a ring, a necklace or an ornament — it's still gold. It's the same with humans; we are always spirits, just taking on another form in another life experience. I tend to liken it to actors in a play. After each play, we take off the clothes for the character and find a new script, then adapt to the new character.

Lots of people are aware now that they can clear their systems and start again, creating a new life. They are starting to see their bodies as a system of energy and therefore understand that energy can transform.

Yes, we can transform our bodies, minds and spirits to whatever we want.

What potential!

Chapter 4

Back to Basics

IN EINSTEIN'S EQUATION Energy = E = MC2, we learn that (E) energy = (M) Mass, times the speed of light (C) squared. All very complicated? It was for me.

I'm sure my school teachers tried to teach me this subject, but as with most things at school I didn't understand once the subject got too complicated I would simply switch off, as I didn't understand the language they were using.

But what this actually tells us is that mass (matter) and energy are the same thing in different forms. We've been taught that every 'solid' object is made up of molecules and that molecules are made up of atoms. Well, these atoms are made up of subatomic particles, which actually means that the chair that you're sitting on isn't solid at all, but is in fact waves of information and energy. A difficult concept to take in, as our brain (our consciousness) really needs to believe the chair is solid, perhaps so we can trust that it will support us when we sit on it.

To look at this a little closer, we'll start at the beginning!

Energy! Sound! Vibration!

This is the basis of creation.

And as this is what we are made of, it's obvious that sound has an effect on our body, mind and spirit. Other translations in the East call this sound 'AUM', which is made up of the vibration AH-OO-MM. So really, we are pure energy in motion.

Actually, every time you say AUM, or chant it, you will increase your system's power, changing and raising your energy as well as balancing it. That's how many people in the East raise their energy, by sitting quietly and chanting AUM. It's been done for centuries with amazing results, yet so many of us in the West have trouble adopting this practice.

As I said earlier, we don't take much notice of our thoughts, we just let them take over our lives and often get confused by them. When this confusion happens, we stop our first thought; it gets wiped out. So we must be clear in our desire before we ask, otherwise the original 'I wish for…' gets cleared and replaced with doubt, therefore creating what's called a self-fulfilling prophecy. After creating this prophecy, we then start the blame game.

Have you noticed that whenever we want something really badly we do a sort of bartering with God?

'Please God, make them okay and I will go to church every Sunday,' or 'I promise to meditate more,' etc.

For those who don't get what was asked for, they quickly remember God's part in it and put all their anger in God's failure. Yet really, he/she/it hasn't even taken part. We started the game in the first place. He/she/it didn't come to us and say,

'I'll give you this if you start coming to church every Sunday.'

More bizarrely, if we happen to bring in the desired wish, we tend to forget about the deal we made.

> '*You are what your deep, driving desire is. As your desire is, so is your will. As your will is, so is your deed. As your deed is, so is your destiny.*' — The Upanishads Spiritual Hindu Scriptures

I suppose God is a little like the parent who sits away from the child while he/she tries to figure out how to do a task. Rather than do it for us, which wouldn't really help the child learn at all, we are left to try to figure it out for ourselves. After all, when we were created we were given free choice, and with free choice comes *responsibility* of thoughts and emotions, as every vibration a human sends out causes a reaction in the cosmic soup of life and affects everything else.

This is a daunting thought, as many of us don't have a clue where many of our 60,000 thoughts each day are heading at any given moment, as every vibration we choose to transmit comes back to us eventually (karma) and we can measure these vibrations by what is happening in our lives.

For example, when a person is too materialistic, the vibrations emanating will come back in equal measures, but when they become more spiritual and send out higher vibrations, these will return three-fold, and when totally spiritual, ten-fold. I suppose this could be what we call instant karma and maybe that's why the spiritual path's so hard to be on, as we know it's even more important to watch our thoughts.

But so many people are not being true to themselves by living the lives they think they should have rather than the lives they truly want. I realise it's scary to be who you know you really are, but don't we owe it to ourselves?

There is a difference in *thinking* you are happy and *feeling* that you are happy!

If we say we feel happy but don't really, the energy sent out from our system will be low, no matter what we are saying. But if we *feel* happy, then the energy sent out from the heart will reflect this.

Just sit quietly for a moment and say this word: *think...*

Then say: *feel...*

Just saying them gives you a different vibration. The key to being in harmony with ourselves is balance; that means not living from the head, but from the heart.

Human behaviour is about habit and imagination, which is far more powerful than logic. Our deepest fear isn't that we are inadequate, but that we are powerful. It's our light, not our darkness that frightens us most. But who are we not to be powerful? Why are we so afraid of success, or being the best?

Unfortunately, it goes back to our programming, as we are often taught that it's vain to think of ourselves in such a high view. But to be honest, there is nothing good about shrinking in a crowd, but we often do it to make others feel better.

We are born to make the most of the energy system that's within us. We are born to fulfil our heart's desires! We are born to shine from within. This simply means showing off our energy field or our aura.

To see a person's energy field glowing to its full potential must be a true treasure, and I thought this especially after I read *Hands of Light* by Barbara Ann Brennan. In her amazing book she shows pictures of what she views daily. It's said that in the future we'll all have this ability and I'm looking forward to it. We will know how a person feels by the colours of their aura (although this will be a little scary for those who are dishonest).

Once we become aware that holding on to our emotions (e-motion = energy in motion) will block this system of swirling energy, we will be in a better position to keep our system clear and healthy. In an ideal world this would be so easy to maintain, but one of the hardest things to learn is not to lose our energy, as we are constantly thinking about our past or our future.

Therefore, we deplete our system, as *where thought goes, energy flows*.

Of the 100% energy we generate daily, the majority goes to our past and some goes to our future; therefore, we try to manifest our wishes and desires on what's left, about 10%. Of course, each individual is different. I know people who are the other way round and think of nothing but the future they desire.

We must learn to watch our thoughts and be in charge of them, instead of our thoughts being in charge of us. This is a very important point, because when we try to create the life we desire our thoughts play a vital role. Tuning into the energy of *our spirit* is difficult until you get the hang of it, just as with everything that is new, but it's so worthwhile when we achieve it, as our life becomes a lot easier. Of course, this can be an alien concept for people who've been brought up to believe they are a victim of life.

Let's take this concept a little further. If you were looking at a radio for the first time and had limited knowledge of how to receive information from the machine, what would you do? You work out that you must turn it on, yet still no sound! You keep on looking at it and finally, you work out how to get a sound from it, but it's not what you want to hear, and is distorted and crackling.

You notice three wavebands and so you turn to each, but all you get is the crackling noise. You finally see the control to tune it in and then a sound comes out of the machine. This may take time, as there are many different stations to choose from and you don't want rock 'n' roll blaring if you're a lover of the waltz. So you must be patient until you find the sound you are happy with.

> '*The things we think are destroyed are now in a frequency that we've tuned out of. The things we think are created have come into a frequency that we're tuned in to, but there is actually no creation or destruction, just change in form.*' – Buckminster Fuller, American Visionary

When we are ready to work with our spirit, we begin with the desire and then make a conscious decision to put the hours in to stay *centred*. Then the responsibility comes, as we must watch our behaviour, not to mention what food and drink we put in our system, as this affects the vibration patterns.

When we look at life from a whole-istic viewpoint, we begin to realise that we are the writers, producers and directors of our own movie, and that at any time throughout the movie we can change scenes, or we can scrap the movie altogether if we are not happy with it and start again; we start drawing new pages.

Similar to the old-fashioned cinema, where a picture was placed on each page and then, when there were enough pictures for the story, you would flick each page quickly, creating the illusion that the figures were moving. You would actually see a scene taking place before your very eyes, as our brain tells us that is the way it is.

It's the same with the way we view life. Some of us think it's real and many other people have a different train of thought: the thought that life could actually be an illusion. I had trouble understanding this concept, but the more I thought about it, the more I thought it could be a good way of viewing things.

Another fact that fascinated me was why we keep creating the same dramas? The truth is, we process information constantly and it's coloured by what we have in our memory bank, by what we remember. We may find that we have opportunities in life, but we do not see them because of our conditioning, as the brain does not differentiate between what it sees and what it remembers.

Once we *know* (and it is the *knowing* part that's often so difficult for us) that everything is energy and that there is absolutely no distinction between matter and energy, the boundaries between the physical world and the world of our thoughts will start to disappear.

Since Einstein's theory, the world of quantum physics has revealed some very interesting things. Physicist Ervin Laszlo wrote a book called *Science and the Akashic Field*, in which he describes a series of experiments conducted by lie detector expert Cleve Backster, in which Backster took some white blood cells from the mouths of some of his subjects and cultured them in a test tube.

He then moved the cultures to distant locations and attached lie detectors to them; he then went on to perform a series of experiments on his subjects. These tests showed that when something emotional was shown to one guy that affected his emotions, the needle on the lie detector miles away reacted, just as if it was attached to the person. WOW! How is such a thing possible?

Could the particles of the person's body still be connected, no matter how far apart they were? Even more bizarre, it is believed that the mere *intention* of measuring particles, even without carrying out the act, would still affect the particles in question! Why do we find this so hard to believe?

If consciousness is what the universe is made of, then matter and energy are just two of the forms consciousness can take. This information is at the cutting edge of science and I believe we will view our world very differently within the next ten years. We will indeed believe that the idea precedes the physical reality.

I had such a fight with myself on this subject. Although I knew this was the truth, bringing it into my reality was so difficult. My children would say to each other when I was in the middle of yet another crisis or illness,

'How can she teach this so well and yet still create crap in her life?'

Simple answer! All my years of programming that everything was 'my fault' and that I have no power to change things! And of course I'm not alone in my thinking!

Being true to ourselves can and does make us feel uncomfortable because of the changes it brings. We tend to ask,

'What if I am doing it wrong?' But there is no wrong; there's no one 'up there' making the rules. Remember, the energy we are made of is:

Feminine = The 'me'. The receiver, and is intuitive.

Masculine = The 'I'. The giver, and is reactive.

The 'me' side of the self (feminine) is made up of a combination of moods, mental states, feelings, likes, tastes and habits.

The 'I' side (masculine) is the being within that can 'will' the 'me' to act according to its wishes, desires and intentions.

Many of us only identify with the 'me' state and feel victimised by its moods.

Both sides need to be balanced in order for us to achieve our full potential.

The feminine side tells our masculine side the ideas and the masculine goes out and gets it for us (this usually brings humour to women, as they say, 'that's how it should be'), but it's the reason why practising giving and receiving daily is healthy for us, as we easily forget to do both. Most people have no problem giving, but receiving is different, usually due to a lack of self-belief and confidence.

Evidence shows this, as in one of my workshops I ask people to write a list of the things they don't like about themselves and they write away merrily. Sometimes, I have to ask them to stop, saying the list is long enough. However, when I ask them to write a list of the things they like about themselves, a very different mood hits the room.

> '*The content of your thoughts and personal beliefs can be proven by a single indicator, your current results.*' – James Arthur Ray

The formation of an atom is due to the clustering of negative electrons around a positive one. They sort of dance around each other and vibrate at a high degree and intensity. When this union starts, the creative process begins.

Whether we use this power or not is our decision, as some people choose to ignore it, while others use it to their advantage and flourish in life. We often find that the 'doers' of the world have more masculine energy and are more action oriented. They tend to know how to get things done, as they're not afraid of taking risks. But they often have trouble receiving, as they don't like to feel vulnerable and often can't relax, or actually do nothing at all.

People that have more feminine energy usually tend to be more relaxed in life, enjoy nurturing themselves and know how to have fun. But they're not very assertive and often find it hard to express their feelings, as they worry about what others may think of them. If we do not understand these two parts of the self, they will do battle within, bringing chaos and taking all our energy. Most destructively, it distracts us from listening to our intuition.

Once we do listen to our intuition, these two parts of the self simply dissolve, as we stop feeding them (remember where thought goes, energy flows). In this balanced state, we can become who we really are, as we're not wasting our energy on:

'I wish I hadn't done or said that last week,' or

'I hope I can get that new house, or job.'

Once we release blocked emotions from the past, a greater flow of energy will enrich our life. But when we hit sadness, anger or guilt, we undo that balance, as our e-motions knock us off keel. Thinking positively isn't the answer, loving ourselves, warts and all, is.

If we always state truthfully what we want, we will not get angry; it's the holding in the feeling that suppresses our energy and leads to anger. As I said earlier, the secret is to be in harmony with both sides of the self.

We simply need to realise that if things are not going the way we want them to, we have to at least start by changing our thoughts, our mental state, as our will directs the attention and then the attention changes the vibration.

So, if you're feeling fearful, don't waste energy trying to kill it. Concentrate on courage and the fear will disappear. Bring in what you *want*, don't feed what you *don't want*. I know it sounds too simple and it isn't always that easy to achieve, as you may be trying to change a lifetime of negative programming.

> '*Every act we perform is a choice, even if we are unaware that we have made a choice. Our unawareness of choice at the level of electrons and atoms gives us the illusion of a mechanical reality. In this way, we appear to be mere victims subject to the whims of a "higher being".*' — Fred Alan Wolf, Quantum Theorist

We are governed by a set of universal laws, which are spoken about in the brilliant film *The Secret*, and also covered in the book *The Spiritual Laws of Success* by Diana Cooper, which help us to understand how the universe works. I don't mean a set of rules (we have enough of those), but a guideline to live by, i.e. what energy we transmit will determine the energy we receive back.

We have hundreds of circuits of energy connecting to us that fuel our body, mind and spirit. This energy feeds us, but if we do not understand how it works and are not careful, we can drain ourselves, literally. When we're feeling low we can even take it from another person, by creating dramas, so they think of us and the situation all the time.

Our responsibility is to take care of our own body, mind and spirit. But our emotions use up most of our supply, usually by us visiting our past. In her great book *Why People Don't Heal and How They Can*, Caroline Myss PhD talks about a very important issue that she calls 'woundology'.

The less energy in our account, the weaker the cell tissues grow — if you do not reverse this pattern, you will be vulnerable to the development of dis-ease, as the body will try to switch on a warning signal for you to notice. Holding on to past events and emotions drains our energy supply Nature is good to us, it shows us something is not right, maybe we're not moving forward, so we get tired, etc. and on it goes if not looked at. That's why forgiveness is so healing, it's like putting down the dead weight you've been carrying for so long, and what a relief when we don't have to keep going over that emotion. That stands for good times too! Illness demands that you turn inward and become conscious of yourself.

This was another turning point for me, as I hadn't realised that thinking of good times was just as damaging as thinking of the pain of my past. I'd found it so hard to stop thinking of when my children were young, or when I was married, or when I could fit into that lovely dress.

When I'd started living alone after all my children had flown the nest, all my old fears seemed to come out of the woodwork. My fear of being alone haunted me, unearthing some unhealthy feelings, which added to the soup of mixed emotions. 'When things were good' is just as tiring and keeps us stuck in the past too, because all we are doing is keeping those emotions alive.

The key is simple, yet doing something about it is hard. The programming's been there for so long and habits can be hard to break. Keep your eye on the thoughts and words you use daily. Try to stay in the NOW, especially with your words, and remember, it's not the past experiences that cause illness, it's holding on to them.

Universal source supplies everything, and it's infinite. To people known as 'sensitive' it's so simple, they just keep observing the signs and believe in synchronicity. To sensitive people, everything shows up when it needs to. They don't ask the source for anything (that suggests something is missing), and when they feel bad, they decide to change the vibration rather than add to an already heavy world.

When we feel good it means we are in alignment and feeling bad simply means we are not, and we can use this information as a barometer. When you wake up, take a few moments to bring your awareness into your body. Tai chi or chi gung are good for this too. Regularly take your shoes off and walk upon the earth, or even hug trees (although many people are uncomfortable with this method).

Also, look at how you breathe.

Is it calm and rhythmic, or jagged, or is it tight and shallow? It doesn't matter how well disciplined you are, if you're not grounded and calm, energy work will be difficult and inaccurate. After all, it's impossible to deal well with life if you are spaced out or not fully in tune with your body.

The centre of gravity of the body is somewhere around the lower belly, where we vibrate our mood. Happy people vibrate in smooth waves and angry people vibrate in jagged waves. Basically, we simply need to get plenty of rest and relaxation, as well as good food, be balanced and most importantly, be true to ourselves, and then the energy field will be strong.

> *'The greatest discovery of my generation is that human beings can alter their lives by altering their attitudes of mind.'* – William James, American Psychologist and Philosopher

Just as a musical note may be reproduced by causing the instrument to vibrate at a certain rate, so, too, can mental states be reproduced at will. In other words, you can control your mental state and lift your vibrations to any level you choose. This concept is only hard to believe when the programming that says it's not possible has been there for a long time.

My intention with this book is to introduce topics and tools to help you understand how the holistic body works. There is a huge selection of reading material around now, as well as the Internet, for more information, which is why I have only briefly touched upon each subject. Please take the subjects further and learn all you can about your ability to create the life you really want.

One day, I hope we'll be teaching our youngsters that they hold the power in their own hands to create the life they want, and that life isn't just the hand they've been dealt.

If we were taught this concept early on in life we could change our 'scenes' when not happy. Maybe then, so many youngsters might not take such drastic measures as drugs, or even suicide.

When a child is born it feels only warmth and security (well, in most cases). Then, as it grows, it starts to see and feel separation in its world and this brings in anxiety. Suddenly, it doesn't get the food, drink or attention it has been getting since birth and this anxiety plays a big part in our learning and growth. It becomes the programming on the disc = Chakra.

But when we start to communicate with our own spirit/soul we can lose that anxiety and realise that we are not separate from anything. We are all interconnected at some level, and therefore no judging, no condemning and no competition is needed. We are all simply having our own experience to take back to the spirit and discuss afterwards, a little like discussing a play when it's over.

If we were taught this in school then we wouldn't end up in some of the situations we face throughout our lives. I often wonder why so many youngsters are 'opting out' of life! Could it be because they know life isn't supposed to be such a struggle (struggle is just a religious programming based on fear – the 'sitting on God's knee' syndrome)?

We have been programmed over the last two centuries to believe that we must do as we're told by others, allowing them to make the important decisions in our life, and we are often told that we must be the best at everything.

I believe the most important thing we should be taught in school is how to believe in ourselves; how to just BE. After all, each one of us is a human BE-ING. Surely, this just means to believe in our self. For me, the most important thing I've learnt on the journey of awareness is to understand what we are made of and why so many 'bad' things happen in the world.

When we understand how or why something has happened, we can make a choice about what we want to do with it. As a child (like a lot of other children in the world), really bad things happened to me that filled me with fear, but somehow I always knew that they were happening for a reason, otherwise 'God' wouldn't let them happen.

I somehow knew I'd be okay and that I would heal from the pain in my life. I didn't know how of course, but inside I had an understanding that it was all happening for a reason.

I can understand if some of you reading this who may still be in pain are not yet in a place to take this to heart; I remember being there myself. I remember throwing *Living Magically* by Gill Edwards into a corner, shouting,

'What does she know? She hasn't gone through what I have in life!'

If this is the case, please be patient with me and with yourself, as it can take a while to get to a place where you will look at the events as learning curves. I also know these words will be tested, especially where painful events are linked to children.

At seminars, etc. I'm asked how I can say things like 'everything happens for a reason', and some say,

'What would you do if this or that happened to any of your family?'

I reply that I'm human; therefore, I would react as anyone would, with emotion.

At some point (and it is individual to each), a light is switched on and things start to be less painful in life. We begin to look at events from a different angle. We begin to see that a physical problem can be treated by finding the REAL reason why it has entered the physical body. Or, if it's an emotional crisis that's causing havoc, we can realise that there will be an underlying problem (root) and this must be found and taken out fully before the situation or problem can be cleared.

Because of the way our system is structured, a physical problem HAS to start in the other 'bodies' first, unless of course a person is born with certain 'defects', in which case it could be the soul's need for that experience.

But if an illness has become a problem, there will be a reason.

Usually, we have made a decision that isn't healthy for us, creating a 'block' in our system, and if we make a different decision we will 'unblock' the area. If we learn to understand the different layers of ourselves, we can usually find a way to clear the dis-ease or illness.

> 'There are three principles in a man's being and life, the principle of thought, the principle of speech, and the principle of action. The origin of all conflict between me and my fellow men is that I do not say what I mean and I don't do what I say.' – Martin Buber, Austrian-Jewish Philosopher and Educator

We must look at the words we use, as our language is very important; it holds a vibration. An understanding of this can help us to see what is going on in our lives. Try to pay extra attention to your language for a while and be aware of the words you use. Remember, *where thought goes, energy flows*; therefore, whatever we give attention to will get larger! Do you find yourself saying, 'My back is killing me,' or 'I can't stand this any longer,' or even 'I'm stupid/fat/skinny'?

Whatever language you use to yourself and others is being programmed into your computer/brain and will be stored, and as your body wants to please your mind, it will conduct itself accordingly. Therefore, the 'I can't stand it any longer' will eventually lead to leg or back problems.

If we learn to use our body as a manual, we can clear up illness or dis-ease ourselves, as the body is self-repairing when energy flows through it freely. I'm not saying there isn't a place for therapists; I'm saying that only *we* can *truly* heal our lives. The therapist is a very important tool in the healing process, as often, when our bodies have worn down or become dysfunctional, our energy field is so low that we just have no energy left to lift ourselves 'up' when we are 'down' (again, look closely at the words used).

I'm aware that I upset many people with my theory on illness, as my friends will say to me: 'Can't you just have a headache like everyone else?'

But I know that my body and what is happening in my life is a reflection of how I 'feel' on the inside and also of how I've been thinking recently.

How you think today will have an effect on your tomorrow's events. Therefore, if my heart is not happy (truly happy), then my world cannot reflect a happy heart. If I'm not happy hearing the words spoken to me, I will not have happy ears, etc. You can often see where your thoughts have been by what's happening in the present.

I understand that some people won't want to take this onboard and that's fine, as everyone has a choice. It doesn't work for everyone, but it works for me and many, many other people I've come across in the past fifteen years. Before you dismiss this theory (as I did when I first came across it), for a short period of time, maybe a week, try to look at your life and body and read what it is saying to you.

Of course, if you are in good health and life is truly happy, then you have nothing to do but congratulate yourself on being true to yourself and leading the life you truly want. However, if you are not well, or life is really tough, then look at the language you use and what part of your body is trying to get a message to you.

While in the process of writing this book I gave myself the perfect opportunity to see how much I believe this theory. I created many problems and began to wonder at one stage if I was creating them due to the fact that I was giving them attention by writing about them. There was one particular problem with my ears; they became very itchy and sore.

I would do the obvious things to relieve the problem by looking to the nearest chakra, as I knew it was linked to communication. I didn't realise it at the time, but I was only playing lip service to getting to the cause of the problem (although in my mind I had done all that was necessary to heal the situation), but to my dismay, the problem came back time and time again.

Eventually, this drove me mad (again, be aware of my language). Mad = anger = heat. Each time the irritation came back it was worse, and the more I gave it attention the worse it became, to the point where it became infected and I couldn't even hold a phone to my ear. I had to visit the doctor a few times, each time seeing a different one and only to be told different advice as to what they thought the cause was.

Not only was I resisting getting to the root of the problem, I was also resisting efforts of clearing it. This created much resentment towards myself for not being able to sort it out and also resentment towards everyone around me.

As my energy got lower, so did my life, and over a period of weeks I started to alienate myself by creating conflicts with almost everyone around me.

I told those in spirit that 'worked' with me to go away, as I didn't want to work with 'energy' any more. I'd had enough and I wanted to go back to 'normal'. I was in fact self-sabotaging myself and everything I'd worked for. Eventually, I forgave myself for needing to call for help and realised what a hard time I gave myself if ever in need of medical treatment. I felt like I was letting the side down by becoming ill in the first place.

'Well, your beliefs can't work that well if YOU are ill, can they?' or 'Those crystals *really* work, don't they,' would be said sarcastically.

It took time, but as my energy lifted a little I was able to see more of the situation and what may have been the root cause of it all. I'd been looking at what had been happening lately linked with communication, when in fact it went much deeper than that.

I'd been overworking to the point of exhaustion and had clearly not <u>listened</u> to my body. I wanted my new shop to be finished before I went to India to run my retreat; I needed to train someone who would manage the shop in my absence; I had a deadline for the book, as I'd missed two previous dates; I was moving house and putting on a show, all at the same time.

'*Fatigue makes cowards of us all.*' – Shakespeare

I'd written the outline of this book with ease, as I was abroad in the sun and enjoyed the thought of it. However, once the publishers accepted me and my idea became manifest, panic started setting in. I started worrying about how it would be received by those I knew, wondering how people would take my words and what people would think of me.

The little hobby was now a job that needed to be finished! It took on a different slant altogether and the ego took over. The frightened, vulnerable little girl came out to play once again.

Through all this, I still could not find the root to the problem of my ear infection, but if you look at the issues shown above, they all link with communication. I looked at the body chart for help and realised I hadn't gone back to the first time it had bothered me. My ego was having fun by bringing back all my childhood fears of what people thought of me, as the conflict with my ears concerned a family issue. I was hearing words within the family that I wasn't happy with and my ears were symbolically crying. The clear liquid weeping from my ears was turning to eczema (eczema is linked to stress/fear).

Putting it all together, I knew the message was that I was scared of an outcome. I knew confrontation was needed at some point and, like most people, I do not like confrontation, so I'd bury the emotion until another day. I would walk away knowing that what had been said had hurt my feelings. The real issue was just that!

I slowly began to realise that they were *my* feelings and mine alone. If what someone has said hurt my feelings then it is I who needs to address the problem. It might be true that someone has said something to hurt me, but it's how I *receive* the words that matters, and depending on how I'm feeling at that moment determines how I receive them.

In other words, if I'm feeling good with myself and a sentence is said it will make me smile, or I may not even hear the offending words. However, if I am feeling low these same words will cut through me and affect my day and therefore my energy field.

Take for instance if I am feeling bad over my parenting skills for whatever reason and one of my children says something that I can take the wrong way. I will play the words over and over again in my head.

Each time I do this, the information is loading on the disc and, as like attract like, I will attract into my day the situation that will test if I have let go of this worry. If I'm having a self-doubt day, events will keep coming up to give me a chance to heal those thoughts within myself.

The way we see ourselves when viewed with 100% honesty is so important. In my heart I know that for the majority of my life I've been a good mother, giving my children the foundations they needed (*from a soul level*). I'm still working on forgiving myself for that percentage where I know I let them down. Any conflict I carry trying to prove I'm a good mother is wasted energy, as a person only sees what they need to see at that time and each issue will be resolved in his/her own time.

With my own situation involving my childhood, I forgave my mother for not being there for me, but it was only after she'd died that I totally understood her. One day I finally walked in her shoes and saw her from a different angle, and that is the only way we can truly understand another person's situation.

Instead of blaming and hating her for not being like other mothers, I finally understood that she could only love me to the best of *her* ability and she did that from within the pain she was living through.

'*Our life is what our thoughts make it.*' Marcus Aurelius,
Roman Emperor and Stoic Philosopher

We become the people we are because of the adults that are part of our life, and because of the way my mother was when I was young (rather bitter and wasting her life) I made sure I wouldn't end up wasting my life. It made me the driven person I am, trying not to rely on others, trying not to be a burden on my children, to work hard, to travel, to literally do all she didn't, but most of all, not to waste my life. So although my mother wasn't the mother I wanted her to be, she was just what I needed to make me who I am, warts and all.

Another thing to remember is that any conflict we have in our hearts will create conflict in our lives, and once we make total peace with our situation we'll find peace in our hearts. Our behaviour reflects what's in our heart and, as with everything, it carries energy to where it is directed. That is why intention and language are so powerful, and so important.

Some of the language we use, without realising what we are actually saying to ourselves or others, affects our lives. Such as:

'You make me feel sick'... 'You're doing my head in'... 'I'm sick of you'... 'You're getting on my nerves'... 'My back's killing me'... 'That's hard to swallow'... 'You're breaking my heart'... 'He/she is a pain in the backside' and 'Give me a break'.

These are just some of the many programmed messages we store and often use on a daily basis, and the mental images we hold are powerful. Unless we change those images our bodies will always follow suit; for example, extreme trauma in childhood may mean we will grow up tall and thin, as if to grow away from our feelings.

The framework (the skeleton) is an expression of who we are in this life, and if we break a bone it represents a very profound situation or conflict within us, indicating a need to make deep inner changes.

Fat can mean fear. If we stop flowing and resist experiences, we can put on weight. Tight firm fat often indicates deep fear and entrenched mental patterns; floppy fat sometimes indicates holding back emotions, or unshed tears. Hips protect our sexuality, or indicate a fear of moving forward. Tendons link the bones of our core self and the mental energy of our muscles. The chart below suggests some of the ailments we may face if programming persists, and the possible cause.

Position in body	Possible suggestion as to cause
Back	Feelings of a lack of support
Legs, Feet and Ankles	Lack of courage to go forward or staying stuck in the past
Knees	Difficulty adapting to change
Thighs	**Outside** – insecurity within themselves. **Inside** – lack of being cared for or could be lack of physical love
Hips	Immobility on any level and narrow-mindedness
Liver	Stuck emotion, often anger can be stored in liver – may go back many years (can be contributor to arthritis)
Pancreas	Feelings of a lack of sweetness in life
Stomach	Can't digest what is happening in life
Lungs	Not open to new ideas or can't express feelings – not taking in full life force
Chest	Need to get something off the chest and make feelings shown. Not proud, need to sink away, make self smaller. Often find this person will have round shoulders
Hands	**Left** – people who cannot receive, due to feeling unworthy. **Right** – wanting to keep things close to the chest
Shoulder/Upper Arm	Too many burdens in life or carrying other people's problems around
Arms generally	Lack of spontaneity or opening up. Trouble giving and taking
Neck	Need to hold head high regardless of circumstances or problems. Not manifesting ideas or supporting thinking
Ears	Not wanting to hear something around them or not manifesting their dreams and desires
Mouth	Need to speak what is inside and express feelings
Teeth	Decision-making
Eyes	Seeing

These and many more parts of the body are examined in greater detail in the fantastic book by Louise L. Hay, *You Can Heal Your Life*, and I highly recommend owning a copy as it's a great reference book. I am always astounded by its accuracy, even down to a cut finger.

If we take the example of a person who is putting on weight for no 'apparent' reason, the obvious thing to do is to look at their food intake, but many people eat little and still gain weight, so this isn't always the cause. Look more closely at the whole situation.

Psychologically, this person could be feeling insecure over a recent situation. There's a good chance the person who's put on weight is in fact holding on to something from the past. The feelings inside may bring up the memory of lack, so 'I need to store for later' may also be there too. Or maybe this person had a childhood of poverty; therefore, when this feeling of insecurity raises itself again years later, the person may automatically eat more so the body can hold on to the fat in the system to be used at a time when it would be called for.

> '*It's a strange thing how human consciousness is so determined to hang on to the past, hold it in the present, and make it reappear in the future. This is the heart of most of our problems.*' — James Arthur Ray

When the insecure feelings arise, this person will often become constipated, another sign of holding on to the past and another reason for weight gain, because if the body does not get rid of waste in the body within 24 hours, the waste will be stored in the body as fat. This in turn causes more feelings of despair and the person goes round in circles of not feeling good about her/himself and so on.

I believe a good point at which to start understanding the body as a whole is with the subtle bodies. A little knowledge of this ancient energy system is better than no knowledge at all, so don't be put off by the vast knowledge that is available to learn.

Let us take a closer look at what these systems are, and how they work!

CHAPTER 5

Auras and Chakras

THE AURA is the life force that surrounds the body and radiates from it. It is electromagnetic and contains many colours, as every thought and emotion reflected in the aura vibrates to a different colour.

Thankfully, scientists are now acknowledging the awareness of energy fields and accept that they can measure the frequency of human energies:

Electrical currents from the heart – electrocardiogram (ECG)

Electrical currents from the brain – electroencephalogram (EEG)

Electrical currents from the skin – known as a lie detector

The most general information on the auric field is that there are seven main layers, each relating to a specific chakra. Chakra is a Sanskrit word meaning spinning wheel, or vortex. These layers vary in density, the closest to the physical body being the densest and the furthest away being the lightest, finest and of higher vibration. Being denser, the lower levels are the easiest to see, but you may be able to see the other layers if you practise.

Try sitting and looking at a person or a plant in the room and continue to stare for a length of time, similar to daydreaming. Then let your focus drift. After a while you may be able to see a sort of haziness around the object, a little like the old-fashioned porridge advert, where the boy had a warm haze around him to keep him warm.

Try this exercise now and see what happens. Perhaps take notes, as it will be good to refer back to these at a later date when you are doing more of this work. You'll see how much easier it becomes the more you practise.

The aura's seven layers flow into each other and each layer is of a higher vibration to the one below, so although they share the same space, they do extend beyond it. Therefore, each layer is a body in itself, lying within another body.

Each layer also has its own particular function, but don't worry too much about remembering these details, unless you are thinking of taking up the subject. The seven layers are:

1. Etheric
2. Emotional
3. Mental
4. Astral
5. Etheric template
6. Celestial
7. Ketheric

The *Etheric* layer is concerned with physical functioning and sensations of the body, and is associated with the automatic functioning of the physical body. This layer has a sort of web-like structure and is in constant motion. It is said to extend ¼–2 inches beyond the physical body and pulsates at about 15–20 cycles per minute. The colour varies from light blue to grey and it relates to the Base or Root Chakra.

The *Emotional* layer is concerned with emotional aspects and roughly follows the outline of the physical body. This layer contains all the colours of the rainbow, from brilliant clear hues to dark muddy ones, depending on the clarity or confusion of the feelings, or the energy that produces them. It extends 1–3 inches from the physical body and is related to the Sacral Chakra.

The *Mental* layer is concerned with mental, linear thinking and is associated with thoughts and mental processes. It often appears as bright yellow, but when a person is concentrating it will expand and become brighter. It extends 3–8 inches from the physical body and contains the structure of our ideas. Thoughts can often be seen in it as shapes of varying brightness and it relates to the Solar Plexus Chakra.

These first three layers are associated with the physical world. The fourth layer, the *Astral* layer, is the one through which energy passes when going from one world to another and 'marries' the two sets together, as layers five to seven relate to the spiritual world.

The *Astral* layer relates to the Heart Chakra and is concerned with love, not romance, but love of humanity in general, and extends about 6–12 inches from the physical body. A great deal of interaction takes place between people on the astral level and can account for feelings of unease when you enter the company of someone and don't feel right, i.e. the energies of the two people are not interacting well, so you tend to fold your arms. Although I have come across others that say this happens on the mental layer, as folding arms protects the Solar Plexus.

The *Etheric Template* layer is connected with the higher will, speaking things into being and taking responsibility for one's actions. Like the Etheric layer, it contains all forms that exist on the physical plane, and is likened to a blueprint or a template. Relating to the Throat Chakra, it is said to extend about 1½–2 feet from the physical body and appears as transparent lines on a cobalt blue background.

The *Celestial* layer is concerned with celestial love, which is beyond human love and encompasses all life. Extending 2–2¾ feet from the body it appears as a shimmering light and looks like mother of pearl. Relating to the Third Eye Chakra, the Celestial layer surrounds the body like a glow around a candle, with brighter beams of light within it.

The *Ketheric* layer is about the higher mind and knowing our spiritual and physical make-up, and it extends 2½–3½ feet from the body. When we think on this level we know we are at one with the creator.

The outer form of this layer is the egg shape of the aura. It is a highly structured template, composing of tiny threads of gold/silver light and is very strong, holding the whole form of the aura together, like a net. Its appearance is golden shimmering lights pulsating very fast, and the outer edge is about ¼–½ inch thick. It also contains the main current that runs up and down the spine, and relates to the Crown Chakra.

It is said that when people form relationships with each other, cords are formed on many levels of the auric fields. The longer and deeper the relationship, the stronger and more of them there are. If the relationship ends, the cords are torn, often causing great pain. This could be where the term 'getting over' comes from, as it refers to the period needed to disconnect the cords and re-root them within the self (we call it pulling yourself together).

Each layer of the aura affects the layer below. When we are true to ourselves, we have a natural flow of feelings. We will then have an increased awareness of our body, which will lead to eating properly and taking appropriate healthy exercise. A healthy mind (mental body) will lead to a healthy emotional body and then a healthy Etheric body and finally, a healthy physical body.

It is necessary to ensure that the balance of energy in the Etheric body is maintained. Coming from a natural flow of feelings this will lead to increased awareness of body sensations. The healthy Etheric body then supports and maintains a healthy physical body, keeping its chemical and physical systems balanced and functioning normally, bringing good physical health. When the physical body is healthy, it will be reflected in the Etheric.

In a dis-eased system, the same step down process is at work, but causing imbalances. As the sensitivity to the body is decreased, it can create a negative loop of more unbalanced energies that will eventually lead to dis-ease.

As our Emotional Body holds our good and bad experiences in our life, it is not only dealing with current events but dealing with unresolved issues too. It's giving out unconscious messages through the chakras and attracting people and events into our lives, making the world a mirror in which we can observe ourselves and our unconscious mind.

Maybe that's why so many people working in the field of healing can seem to have so much chaos in their lives, as they are working with energy, highlighting these subjects and clearing old issues.

It's very important to have a healthy subtle body, as it maintains a healthy physical body and so on. So, knowing all this information, how do we keep our aura healthy? Crystals, Reiki and many other therapies exist to help us keep our energy intact, but I still firmly believe that if we respond to our own needs each day, and listen to and read our body, mind and emotions, our energy will reflect this. In other words, love ourselves and give ourselves TLC daily.

The chakras are also part of the subtle anatomy system. People's views and descriptions of the subtle bodies and the chakras differ, according to whom you ask. They are a vortex of energy and are referred to as wheels. Traditionally, they have been symbolised by a lotus flower and you may come across many variations of the chakras and a difference of opinion, but a common viewpoint is as follows:

There are seven major chakras, each relating to an organ of the body, a gland and an aspect of the personality. They appear at the back and the front of the body and appear more complex as they move up the body, the Crown being the most complex, the Base being the most dense and simple. Each chakra resonates to a colour and a note on the musical scale, which is how colour and music can heal the body. The basic functions of the chakras are:

1. *The Base* or *Root* (at the perineum) relates to our ability to connect with the earth, and it governs our functions in the physical world. Our

survival needs are here, as well as issues of security, food, money, jobs, etc. This rules the adrenals and vibrates to the colour red, the note C and the sense of smell. So, a problem with the legs could relate to a money or job issue, wondering if we can survive, etc.

2. *The Sacral* (below the belly button) relates to relationships, creativity and sexual energy, the spleen, reproductive/sexual energy and the colour orange, the note D and the sense of taste. A problem with ovaries or testicles could relate to an issue with relationships.

3. *The Solar Plexus* (above the belly button and under the ribcage) relates to mental ego, personal power, confidence and will (willpower), the pancreas and upper stomach, the colour yellow, the note E and the sense of sight. A problem with the stomach may reflect not wanting to digest something that is happening in life and you may feel you have no confidence to deal with it (this is also where what is known as our inner child resides, and it's where we hold onto hurt feelings as a child and also where we store so many of our memories). Our inner child is the child part of our spirit and higher self, like the guardian.

4. *The Heart* (centre of the chest) relates to the ability to give and receive love and it governs the physical heart, lungs and skin, and relates to feelings of compassion, the colour green, the note F and the sense of touch. This chakra links to all our fears too; so many problems in the chest area could relate back to fear of some kind. It is also where we store grief, anger, resentment, jealousy and guilt (all part of fear).

5. *The Throat* (in the throat) relates to all forms of communication (including the ears), expressing thoughts and feelings freely, and bringing into reality what we want to manifest in our life. It rules the thyroid, parathyroid and the colour blue, the note G and the sense of sound. Problems here could be not being heard or not wanting to hear what is really going on around us.

6. *The Third Eye* or *Brow* (in the middle of the eyebrows) relates to intuition and light. It rules the pituitary gland, the colour indigo, the note A and vision. Problems here such as headaches could be to do with not trusting our own hunches, etc.

7. *The Crown* (top of the head) is the centre of knowledge and wisdom, and the receiving point for healing energy. It relates to the pineal gland, the colour purple, the note B and wisdom. Problems here often link with having lost our faith in something.

This is basic information and you may even find it contradictory to other teachings that are around, but don't worry, just trust yourself as you go along. The most important point is the main purpose of the chakra, which is to take in energy, process it and give it out, and that is what it does. The way energy is processed depends on the state of the person at the time. So you can see that if a person is only looking at issues to do with money and is working on nothing more, then the energy of this person will stay in the lower chakras.

When we hear the word negative, we automatically think that means the energy is bad, but we need to get past that idea, as we need negative energy as much as positive. We just need to learn how to get a balance of both. The imbalance could have a lot to do with our religious history, as we've been programmed for a very long time to not use these vortexes. Told that they were only for the chosen few, such as heads of state, church elders and monks, etc., made it difficult for those who knew different to be able to discuss such things and forced the teachings to go underground. Thankfully, a thread of all this knowledge was stored in such things as tarot cards and fairy stories (see Archetypes, Chapter 6).

> 'When the intention is clear, the outcome will appear.'
> James Arthur Ray

If a person's attention only focuses on the lower centres, they will 'feed' them, as remember, where thought goes, energy flows. They will feed these issues and without realising, as they are attracting people and things of similar energy. So, they will go to places that have the same vibration relating to work, food, money and so on. Also, remember that a worry about a lack of something is often where thoughts are, which will also keep the negative loop going.

Someone who works with the higher chakras might have healthy, strong, higher centres, therefore attracting those that are similar to them and joining groups with similar minds, etc. The issues that will be strong are creativity, intuition and maybe 'heavenly' subjects. You might find that they have their head in the clouds, or are 'on another planet'.

This can often happen when a person starts looking into the subjects of angels, crystals or meditation and nothing else, as they tend to forget about earthly matters. They have to learn how to walk with 'a foot in both worlds', as Gill Edwards terms it, and I think that sums it up well.

When I first got into the subject of crystals I often didn't know which 'camp' I belonged to and would fight myself on how I should act, look and even dress, as the people I met daily were so different from those in my life.

When I started to change, I missed the people in my regular life and fought myself to get back to being 'normal', which brought a real struggle within and for a long time I wanted to forget about this kind of thing. Sometimes even now, I can find myself still wanting to. This could also explain why there is such a divide between people who believe in spiritual subjects and those who don't, as they don't understand each other's thinking.

Do we need to be in balance all the time? I don't think so. The secret is to let life *flow* continuously and enjoy the flow as it goes *through* us; feeling every grain as it passes through, feeling every emotion as it flows along. After all, *this* experience will never be repeated. This is a *unique* moment! Although we'll have similar experiences, each one is *unique* in some way.

To find out what is happening in your system at this moment, all you need to do is to look at your body. For instance, if your ear is sore, what might you not want to hear? If it's constantly itching, ask what it is that you're hearing that is annoying you so much. Or maybe the ear is inflamed? Inflammation = heat = anger.

It will be something to do with communication, or bringing what you desire into your life. It could also be about not expressing your feelings freely, or maybe not taking full responsibility for the events in your life, as that's what the communication chakra represents.

As each chakra links with a layer of the aura, e.g. the throat chakra relating to the Etheric Template layer, it will link in some way to taking responsibility for one's actions and speaking things into being.

For any problem, find the chakra that's nearest to the part of the body that is causing the problem and look to see what its function is linked to; also look to the layer of the aura and the archetype, and then you will eventually find the reason for the imbalance and what it's trying to tell you.

If it's already a problem within the physical body, then it must have been around in the other layers first, so look back to a few weeks before the physical problem started. See what your thoughts and emotions were like, and this will give you an idea of the area to look. But although you may pinpoint the cause, it may take a little time for a block to clear completely, as it has to go through the step down process.

Let's take a problem with fear that's been around for a while, such that it will probably have entered the physical body. It could be affecting the physical heart, lungs or skin, and even after you have found the cause and sorted it out, it then has to move back through the layers it came from. Once you are honest with yourself and identify the problem, you will become aware of the *real* issue causing the physical problem.

Time-lining is a technique that helps us root out a problem. You'll need a pen, paper and some quiet time so you can think about the issue you are going to 'root' out.

Look at the problem you are facing (if more than one, take the oldest one first, as this often roots and clears more easily than a more recent issue). Don't spend too long thinking about it, though, as you may get lost in memories and that will defeat what you are trying to achieve.

When you have identified what you are going to work through, notice how it makes you FEEL, for example *useless, hopeless, daft, lonely, worthless*.

These won't include such labels as *frustrated, annoyed, disappointed*, as these are *results* of a deeper feeling.

When you have written down the feeling, date it as near as possible, i.e.

2007 – Powerless

Then sit and think back to a time before this date when you felt powerless.

2006 – ....

Repeat again.

2005 – ....

And so on. Work your way back until you know it was the first time you felt that way.

You may find that you will go back to early childhood with this, and if this is so, it's more likely to be something you have come into this world to experience and learn from. When you have found the root, light a candle and say a blessing of some kind. Something like: *I release and set free these memories, thanking them for the learning I have received. I release them with love to all concerned. I will it so, so be it. Amen.*

Then, in a safe environment, set light to the paper and set it free. Release it. Let it go. You no longer need it in your life. Thank it as you let it go, as it has served you well; it has served its purpose. As you blow out the candle, send the light to the past. If it's possible, shower afterwards, once again affirming that you have released this old pattern and are ready to live life anew from this moment onwards.

I recently had great reason to look at this in practice. I'd had a really painful stomach problem, which I couldn't seem to clear, until I realised that a couple of weeks previously I had given my power away so many times and I didn't have the confidence to stand up for myself. Once I had realised where the problem came from, it began to heal.

When you start to be aware of the chakra system, you can certainly use the information to your advantage.

Understanding that if your system is in harmony, your life will bring more health, wealth and happiness is rather empowering, too. But unfortunately, a lot of people are going through the motion of living and just waiting for the next bad thing to happen. It doesn't have to be that way!

There are many ways to learn how to use the chakras and as long as you find a good class/teacher, or read up on the subject, then you should be okay.

Over the years I have found that many people have decided to go into the complex subject of mediumship/clairvoyance and the like without having any knowledge of the chakra system. Personally, I don't think that's very responsible. After all, how can you start to learn how to use the third eye (for clairvoyance) or the throat chakra (for clairaudience) without knowing how they work?

It's like driving a car without having any driving lessons.

As I have said earlier, you don't have to be the seventh son of a seventh son to be a healer, or to be a clairvoyant. Clairvoyance simply means clear seeing, clairaudient = clear hearing and clairsentient = clear sensing.

We can all train ourselves to one of the above states of awareness, although some have it naturally, especially today, when so many are 'switching on' automatically. It all depends on our consciousness and our system. If our chakras are healthy and vibrating at the correct speed for these things to happen, then they will if that's what we desire. However, if we do not want to use it, then we can switch it off/close it down.

If it's not working and we desire it to, it simply means that the chakra is having difficulty spinning (as in the case of a wheel when it is clogged with dirt until it is cleaned).

As the information in our chakra is often from the distant past, we often don't know what has caused the blockage, or how to clear it. We'll have literally forgotten what information is logged, and because our energy is low at that point we cannot raise our vibration to search for the cause, never mind a solution.

When it feels too hard to do, we stay in that low energy with the events in our day just mirroring how we are feeling, therefore reinforcing our beliefs that 'all this' doesn't work. That's where the therapist is greatly needed. I work with this information on a daily basis and yet I can be swallowed up in a loop of self-destruction if I'm not aware of what's going on in my life.

So I can understand how someone who has just found this way of thinking can drop it rather quickly when things go wrong. Faith can be quickly lost when after calling on Spirits, Guides and Angels to help they don't seem to appear.

It's important to keep your energy healthy by being part of nature for instance, as we take our energy from the environment around us. It's easy to see why we feel better when we go to a beach, as the beach gives off negative ions from the sea and the sand is mainly quartz, which raises vibrations.

I think it's easy to see how living in inner cities and high-rise flats isn't so healthy for us physically, mentally or spiritually and why many people in these areas have lost any hope of a happy, healthy lifestyle, as once hope is lost, the 'will' to be happy often goes with it (remember that the 'will' is in the solar plexus and it's the chakra that relates to our confidence and self-esteem).

Also, swapping energy has a huge effect on our bodies if it's not healthy. Take two people in an argument. Person 'A' is really angry and therefore sending really angry vibes to person 'B'. It's not hard to see how this has an effect on person B. Then, if we take the situation where another person is involved, person B will be bombarded with even more angry, harsh energy, and if person B has low self-esteem, this energy will go straight into the solar plexus location.

Vulnerable person B will also be affected by the energy of the location, as we get energy from the area we are in at the time. This is another reason why crystals are so important, as they hold and amplify energy. Crystal therapy can help clean out the old stuff no longer needed and bring in new fresh energy that will move us into new areas. This could be why many people report that their life has changed 'by coincidence' since wearing a crystal or since having a treatment.

We now know a great deal about the seven major chakras within the body area, but there are also minor chakras within and outside the body and more information is available for those of you who would like to take this fascinating subject further.

Once our higher chakras start coming into play, we discover that life is not the same, as they hold lifetimes of information and these new systems will help us to clear out what is no longer needed. It's also said that the beams of light within the chakras are in fact coded information, holding a geometric form of language, and as these begin to activate, the new information will come in and settle in our system.

We only take in the information we need and when the time is right. So, for those who feel this is too 'far out', don't worry, you probably won't even notice this information, or if you do, you will quickly forget it.

Our chakras bring information and with it come behavioural patterns. We behave one way when they are in balance and another way when they are not (also known as archetypes). This information is well known in the tarot teachings, but not so much in the West.

Since I started studying the patterns of behaviour, I have found it very helpful for both my clients and myself. I believe that having and understanding this information can help us to understand our lives and the crises we often face.

There are teachings around that say in the future (between 2006 and 2012) our DNA will actually start to change to a 12-strand, which is what humans were at the beginning of time. This could probably help us hold more light in our system for the next phase of evolution. What a fascinating thought!

A friend in New Mexico also suggested that's why children are now suffering from certain behavioural problems; they are wired up differently to be able to accommodate the new frequencies in the air due to phone masts, etc. An interesting concept, I must say!

A DNA with more strands would mean we could move beyond our own self-limitations, beyond the physical body (which many can do already), and use all of our energy to go into the non-physical worlds. Of course, before this can happen we need to look at personal responsibility = throat chakra (this could explain why so many are having a hard time with all forms of communication) and begin to be kind to ourselves by taking proper care of our bodies. Also, when we start to develop the chakras further, we go through many changes and this can bring even more problems. We move away from our old views and ways of life, and this creates more fear. Nothing we try seems to work for us any more, and some of us go through these stages more than once.

It does seem to be up to each of us how we deal with this stage, but it is unhealthy to keep fighting it. I should know; I've been trying to stay the 'same old me' for a long time and when that didn't work I tried to take those I love with me into my new thinking, but that didn't work either.

Thankfully (as always happens), I came across the right book at the right time and realised what I was going through was all part of my learning curve. I suppose consciousness is all about coming to terms with who we are, and where we're going with our own individuality. Carolyn Myss describes in her book *Why People Don't Heal and How They Can*:

> '*More often than not, we are met on our new journey with opposition, as the tribal instinct is to discourage people straying too far. But often our journey of self-discovery begins without us being aware of it, which is probably best, as if we knew what was coming we would not bother.*'

Signs that self-discovery has begun:

 ✻ Discomfort with environment

 ✻ Can't identify depression, tiredness or loneliness

 ✻ Know you want to go forward, healing, etc.

 ✻ Feeling it will never end

 ✻ A shift in time – even healing speeds up

 ✻ An allergy to certain foods and fabrics, etc. especially wheat, dairy or caffeine

 ✻ A new identity – wanting to move away

 ✻ A need for nature

 ✻ The development – often illness that doesn't respond to allopathic medicine procedures

It's what I call 'the dark night of the soul'.

Not all illnesses are the result of negativity in our lives. Maybe it's to do with genetics and our environment, which has a large part to play, but most often, people's lives change because of illness, or an accident (in my life it certainly did). Or maybe we need the experience of looking after someone to be able to see the illness from a different point of view. Maybe we simply need a change in our direction in life

Self-love is about taking care of ourselves and being true to the self, or, as I heard Oprah Winfrey call it, being 'self-full'. The biggest change seems to be deciding that no one else will abuse you in any way. In other words, to respect the self and be happy in life, enjoy it = (in joy).

If you knew that one of your purposes here on earth was to face one of the archetypal behavioural patterns, wouldn't you look at your illness/situation in a different way? If you needed to face your 'victim', wouldn't an illness be the perfect way of doing it? The feelings that you would have to deal with would be a great way to get to the core of the problem. I say *feelings* not *thoughts*, as it's the feelings that will tell you where the root of the problem is.

Each time you look at the feelings, sit with it for a moment and change that feeling to one that makes you feel good, more in power with your situation, and try to do this daily. Eventually, you will have fed the *stronger* you, instead of the *ill* you.

What I often do is sit and pretend I'm another person telling 'me' what the problem is (as if I were a customer coming into the shop seeking my advice). Then I would be receiving the advice I would normally give another person. That way, I could see the whole picture, and from a higher point of view.

Try this, but be HONEST with yourself.

Write down what you have issues with. Now look at your answers and see the archetypes connected. See what you can do to bring changes, and remember, the more time and attention we give ourselves the better. After all, we think nothing of spending endless hours getting to know a new job or partner and yet many of us haven't a clue about who we are. Maybe that's what Christ meant when he told us 'to know thy self'.

A quick view chart for the purpose of the chakras: balance. Visualising the colour, or using/wearing that colour, will help 'feed' it.

Chakra	Colour	Issue
Crown	Purple	Selflessness
Brow	Indigo	Emotional expression
Throat	Blue	Expression
Heart	Green	Compassion
Solar Plexus	Yellow	Self-esteem
Sacral	Orange	Social behaviour
Root	Red/black	Standing up for self

In one school I was taught that each chakra has an age that comes into play, but in another school I was taught something completely different.

However, I'm going to include a little information about the age of the chakra since I feel it's relevant, as if we have a bad experience at a certain age of the chakra, this affects its condition later on in life.

Between the age of:

1–8: the base chakra is coming into play and learning to stand up for the self

8–14: learning about social conditioning

14–21: learning self-esteem and confidence

21–28: about forgiveness and compassion

28–35: about personal expression

Then we go on to learn about emotional expression and selflessness (wisdom). We will have developed our energies well and be armed to face adulthood and be a 'balanced' human being! But what if we haven't had an easy life?

Say, for instance, that a child is abused at the age of seven years; it will not have learnt to stand up for itself properly, and its learning and views of life in this area will be warped. So the child may carry on in life with a few problems, and when he/she gets to thirty-five, more problems may come into their life that can then teach them how to stand up for themselves.

If the same child had had a problem at eighteen as well as seven, at thirty-five they would go through the problems relating to standing up for the self, and when that was sorted they might find they were facing problems linked with self-esteem and confidence. See how it works?

Our energy seems to loop through the chakra that we need to focus on balancing at that time. It would appear that we need to go through this system until we have learnt all we need to learn to balance our system and become the 'wise one'.

This would certainly explain why some people have an easy life and others have a tough one.

CHAPTER 6

Archetypes

ARCHETYPES are patterns that we have been programmed with to help us learn about our behaviour. When we are in balance we behave in a certain manner, which is a healthy archetype, and when we are out of balance we behave differently. Here are some basic suggestions for understanding our archetypal behaviour and the importance of why we act on or re-act to certain situations.

The Crown
Healthy Archetype: The Guru is:
Someone who trusts the universe to provide what is needed in their life. A person who takes responsibility for events in life; one who isn't always asking why when things go wrong, as they have an understanding that life events are from within and not from an outside force. It's someone who has a disciplined meditation practice and allows the spirit to work with them, and they have a respect towards *all* life.

Unhealthy Archetype: The Egotist is:
Someone who doesn't have a good connection with Mother Earth. They blame others for their actions and refuse to be responsible for their thoughts and actions.
It could be someone who is hung up on status and doesn't see themselves as an individual. Life can be seen as meaningless and with no purpose or faith in Spirit or the God/Goddess when in this state of imbalance.

The Brow
Healthy Archetype: The Intuitive is:
Someone who trusts their intuition and is self-aware. They don't allow negativity to run their lives and learn to live in the moment. They also know there is no such thing as an accident, as they understand that thoughts are very powerful. This is someone who allows life to unfold with its ups and downs, is able to love themselves warts and all, and has learnt to forgive

others as well as themselves.

Unhealthy Archetype: The Intellectual is:
People that can be left-brained, overly opinionated and worry all the time. They have trouble turning the mind off and rarely relax. Also, everything must be proven or it's not believed to be true.

The Throat
Healthy Archetype: The Communicator is:
Someone who is able to speak from the heart, giving it a voice, as well as understanding that being yourself inspires others. Walking your talk is vitally important. They are in touch with one's intuition and act upon it. They have faith in the 'unknown' and are comfortable surrendering to a higher power and following their heart/gut/intuition.

Unhealthy Archetype: The Silent Child is:
Someone who is afraid of self-expression and doesn't show hurt feelings or pain, allowing emotions to stagnate in the body due to them not being given a 'voice'. They can often be overweight, as they are unable to let go and express the self honestly. They could have trouble crying and feel that no one loves or cares for them, and they might have been told as a child to be quiet, or that children should be seen and not heard.

The Heart
Healthy Archetype: The Lover is:
Someone who doesn't show wounds. They are not used as a crutch or an excuse to stay stuck in the past. They are compassionate and non-judgmental of others and are in balance with all they do, including diet and exercise.

Unhealthy Archetype: The Actor/Actress is:
Someone who says everything is okay when it is clearly not. They could be starved of love, but do not how to get it, and afraid of intimacy with another person. They rationalise emotions instead of owning/feeling them, and can often sabotage relationships. They cannot let old emotional wounds heal. Sometimes, they close the heart so that they don't have to feel. They can be frightened of losing control and often have co-dependent relationships. They project emotional baggage on to a partner, but will not admit this.

Solar Plexus
Healthy Archetype: The Warrior is:
Someone who is able to live on their own and develop the inner voice. They can make healthy decisions and like/love the self. They have blind-

faith (you know without knowing how you know).

Unhealthy Archetype: The Servant is:
Someone who has no self-confidence and is unable to stand up for what they believe in. Their willpower is often weak, they are easily swayed by others and will attract people who disrespect them, so fulfilling self-destructive tendencies.

Sacral
Healthy Archetype: The Emperor / Empress are:
People who know when enough is enough; they appreciate the finer things in life and are friendly and open. Life is seen as fun and they live it to the full.

Unhealthy Archetype: The Martyrs are:
People who have a negative attitude towards life and are concerned about what others think. They lack creativity and their vitality / energy is low, and they perhaps sleep longer in order to recharge their physical energy.

Base
Healthy Archetype: The Mother is:
Someone who uses all the senses, which are fully operational and utilised. They have a passion for living life to the full and have a good connection with Mother Earth. They treat others with the respect they would like to receive, take responsibility for the self (non-victim) and can manifest dreams / goals.

Unhealthy Archetype: The Victim is:
Someone who is unable to manifest things on the physical plane. They are often unable to keep their word and feel victimised by society. Life is a constant drudge for them and they are often passionless.

Look at some of the fairy stories passed down through the ages, and fictitious characters such as Cinderella and Sleeping Beauty. Can you see their archetypes? Take a while and think about how many archetypes you can think of. Write them down, as this will help you start to think about behaviour patterns in yourself and others.

This information may not seem important, but once we have the knowledge, we can see the patterns of behaviour in ourselves. Mind you, we tend to see them more easily in others, as no one likes to think of themselves as a martyr or a 'poor me', so we find ourselves pointing it out to others. But try to remember that we all mirror each other.

So, if you find someone acting as a 'poor me', ask yourself if it's a reflection, i.e. are you being the 'poor me', or is it showing you that you used to be this way and how far you have come in your own growth?

On my travels I spent many hours looking at this subject and how I had carried out these behaviour patterns with my family and friends. I quickly realised which type of behaviour I was in at a particular situation in my life. I then thought about history and the information we are fed from birth, which makes up our belief patterns.

It's not our fault we don't know this; we can only take in the information we are given. After all, our parents and teachers in life can only pass on the knowledge they were given, and children can only learn by example and programming.

One December morning in 2004, while in India, I woke at 5 a.m. and with no sleep left in me I turned on my computer and started thinking about this subject. Suddenly, what I call the 'surge' happened (this is where I get a burst of heat, like an internal flush), so I turned off my computer and sat quietly, waiting for the 'energy' to come in.

Information started coming in and in my mind I could 'see' a Christmas tree and the Christmas story calling for joy to the world.

I sat for a while wondering why this was coming to me and started thinking how it isn't right that the church calls out the message for giving in the world when the churches and temples seem to be so rich with gold statues. I could never understand how they just didn't dress down the churches and help the poor of the world. After all, Jesus had no riches, and if it's his teachings the church is following, surely they should be leading by example.

I'm not anti-Jesus; in fact, I've always had a deep love for Jesus. But even as a child I couldn't understood how he could be the *only* son of God. I used to think, what about me? How could God have only one son if we are all his children?

These and many more questions would run round my mind as I sat in RE when I was young. But I never wanted to show my conflict, as I thought it would look as if I was disrespecting his teachings, so I just accepted it all.

Of course I'm a lot older now and although I still love the stories of the Nativity, etc., I now believe that that's what they are — stories just changed to suit those who told them. I feel bold saying that and I mean no disrespect to those who find comfort there, but it cannot be possible for those tales to be completely accurate, especially in today's climate when a lot of the teachings that preceded Christianity are around for us to learn from.

'According to your beliefs, it is done unto you.' Matthew 9:29

The most important thing for me to learn was that Jesus possibly went to India to learn the Buddhist way and that so many of his sayings were actually quoted by Buddha long before Jesus was born. It's also said that Jesus was a reincarnated Bodhisattva (enlightened one), that his birth was awaited by members of the Buddhist order and that the three wise men who followed the star were members.

Then there's the monastery at Qumran, near the caves where the Dead Sea Scrolls were found. The theory is that by the time Jesus was three he would have been in danger from Herod, who was very worried about the Essenes, as they challenged his rule. So they took him away to places such as Egypt and India to be taught the Buddhist way and when he returned he was an adult, as well as a Reiki healer. I love this theory.

I came across a great book while I was in India called *Jesus Lived in India* by Holger Kersten. It's about Jesus' life before and *after* his crucifixion (a very controversial subject). I was fascinated at such a thought and one day mentioned it to a friend who was from Kashmir. To my astonishment, he wasn't surprised at all; he said it was common knowledge that Jesus lived to an old age as a holy man and many people had seen his scars.

I asked 'upstairs' why I was told this, and in my mind's eye I was shown the archetypal information of how we are programmed to hold and carry. We pass on such information to the next generation. For example, Santa's red suit was green until a certain drinks company decided he was to wear red and white, and has been red and white ever since. So, if you asked a child now what Santa wears, they would say red and white.

I still didn't understand why I was being shown all of this, so I made myself a coffee and sat for a long time thinking of the whole religious 'thing'.

Even as a child I knew I had an issue with some of the religious things I was taught in school. We were told we must be good, and if we were not, we would go to Hell. My friends of the Catholic faith were told they had to go to church and confess their sins to the priest. My way of thinking was that if God is love and love is in our hearts, then surely 'He' could see and *feel* everything we've done.

So why did they need to go to the priest who could then tell God?

As I sit here writing this section, I have a small plaque of Jesus above my bed and I'm listening to Buddhist music through which I connect to my 'God'.

Later, I'll open up the file containing the teachings of the Kabala.

What a mix!

But I now think that's how it is.

There are many ways to reach our own God, our own Truth.

All of the subjects in this book I have come across along the way, and they sit comfortably with *me. They're what work for me*! They don't belong to any one club as such, as each is from a different place or 'God'.

One day in India, I was attempting a conversation with the Hindu boy who was cleaning my room (on his hands and knees with a rag, may I add). He saw my small plaque of Jesus that I always take on my travels. He put his hand on his heart and said, 'Oh, your God'.

I nodded and he tried in broken English to explain to me that it's his God too, and told me that there are many temples to God all over India. I was trying to explain that I'd seen many of them, but it was difficult for him to understand me, as the language barrier was high.

However, we got over it eventually and proved that communication is possible if wanted enough by both parties; the reason we got over the problem was that we wanted to overcome it and wanted to converse in this important issue. I really enjoyed watching him trying to show his feelings with gestures and sign language when needed, as he didn't have the words to express what he wanted to convey.

The India I found was a very basic culture, but they didn't make me feel that they were poor, as they are always cheerful and always have a huge smile for you. My hometown would be so much richer if we could get people to smile as much as they do in that 'poor' country. And they are not false smiles either; they are from the heart!

I've travelled to many places in the last few years and have found that each area has its own truth about what God is. Surely they can't all be wrong! Of course, it's great that the churches and temples of the world are beautiful, but it can't be right when so many people have no food or place to live.

Religion is causing so much conflict in our world and for me that it doesn't make sense that a person who cannot feed his family in India can be made to pay for paint to make their church look beautiful, which was the case in the village I was in.

I hope that someday this will change and that the true message from Jesus will be taught how it should be, with simplicity and without all the grand riches and rituals.

My belief is that Jesus was and still is a very special soul who, like all the Masters, came into the world to teach us a way of life that would lead us to God. Surely that means to really find our true selves; to make bonds, not ties; to love, not hate; to forgive, especially ourselves; and to heal ourselves before we heal others.

He gave us the example and the tools to do this, but my belief is that we are blinded by the stories handed down by people who I believe actually knew the real truth. But if everything is as it should be, as many teachings say, then maybe it's for us to look beyond what we're being fed and to question things, not just swallow what's given.

Simply to ask ourselves: Does what I'm told feel right?

And if it doesn't, don't swallow it.

Maybe the secret was to go in search of our truth and earn it, rather than be lazy and be given someone else's truth on a plate.

> '*Whatsoever you ask when you pray, believe that you have received it, and you shall have it.*' Mark 11:24

I've come across many books since my thirst for knowledge began, and last year I came across one called *Invisible Realities* by Ronald Wright, in which he states that the 'Bible is indeed a bestseller, but how many people have actually read it?' A good point I thought!

At first, I had trouble believing what I was reading in Ronald's book, but you can make your own mind up if you read it, as I did. That book and many others are around now showing that the Bible teachings may not be too accurate, and that they were misinterpreted when they were translated from Greek to English.

Teachings show now that there was a troublesome minority that split into three main groups – Orthodoxy, which believed Jesus was divine through and through; Arien which believed Jesus had a dual nature, both divine and human; and Jesuit, which believed that the spirit spoke through mediums. The bishops of these three factions were constantly bickering and ex-communicating with each other, which posed a threat to the unity of the empire as a whole, something which Constantine was determined to have at all costs. Then, at the Council of Nicaea, Constantine made Christianity the state religion. Political factors established Christianity, which was proven by the fact that, throughout his life, he worshipped the Greek God Apollo. Only as he lay dying did he ask to be baptised a Christian.

Another interesting concept that has recently come to the surface is that Mary Magdalene was the lover or wife of Jesus (or Yeshua) and that she was the 13th disciple. I have read many books on this fascinating subject, including one called *The Magdalene Legacy* by Laurence Gardner, which gives much factual detail on the subject. But the Church won't hear of it and that is understandable, as they do not want to think of the 'Goddess energy' and the power behind such a concept.

I learnt a lot as I met up with different people from each country I visited; from Mexico to Australia I had many discussions on ancient beliefs and was surprised to find so many books on the subject of how religion was created. I was really shocked when I found that other cultures have a virgin birth and a crucifixion. Also facts such as:

✳ Halos (like most Christian symbology) were borrowed from the ancient Egyptians' sun worship.

✳ Christians celebrate 25th December as Jesus' birth, but according to some, Christ was born in March.

✳ Christmas Day is the ancient pagan holiday of Sol Invictus – unconquered sun = winter solstice, a time when the sun returns and the days get longer.

✳ Even Christ dying isn't exclusively Christian, as the young man dying to absolve sins of his people appears in the earliest tradition of Quetzalcoatl and the Egyptian Horus.

✳ Christian canonisation is taken from ancient 'God-making' rite of Euhemerus.

✳ The practice of 'God-eating', or Holy Communion, is from the Aztecs.

✳ There is also a good resemblance to Zeus when we see the old man with a beard being portrayed as God and even the lone dove is a pagan symbol for the Angel of Peace.

When hearing or reading these facts, I remember being really amazed by the hidden information, as I'd never heard of such things as going against Church teachings. How could I have been brought up believing this when we have written accounts contradicting it, and I wondered why no one had ever made this information available?

Of course it was available, but not to the masses.

People are now changing, and fast.

They want to know what makes us tick, where we are from and where we go next on the journey called life. Subjects are now brought together instead of separated.

Scientists can measure and understand that we are made up of energy and that this energy holds information. Therefore, there is certainly more to us than meets the eye!

Healthy		Unhealthy
Trust, takes responsibility for self, meditates	●	Blames, has no faith, not an individual
Self-aware, lives in the moment, can forgive, knows thoughts are powerful	●	Left-brained, over-opinionated, worries all the time, everything has to be proven
Walks their talk, has faith in higher power, in touch with intuition	●	Afraid of self-expression, doesn't show hurts, was always told to be quiet
Compassionate, in balance, non-judgementa	●	Rationalises emotions, won't feel them, sabotages relationships, closes heart
Can live alone, makes healthy choices, loves the self	●	No self-confidence, can't stand up for self, weak willpower and easily swayed
Lives life to the full, knows when enough is enough	●	Concerned what others think, lacks vitality, sleeps longer to recharge energy
Uses all senses, can manifest goals, good connection to the earth	●	Can't manifest, can't keep their word, feels like a victim, life's a constant drudge

CHAPTER 7

Energies of the Earth

THE EARTH is a huge magnet that generates a massive energy field that's constantly changing. A ley-line is a vein in the earth that has energy running through it.

Geopathic Stress is the earth's vibrations rising up, which, by weak electromagnetic fields created by subterranean running water, certain mineral concentrations, fault lines and underground cavities can become distorted and abnormally high, and therefore harmful to living organisms.

It seems that standing stones, stone circles, churches with graveyards (all places of power) and many churches seem to be dotted along these ley-lines and were also built over ancient pagan holy places.

Throughout history many of these places were known as mysterious, with doorways leading to fairies and elves, etc. and in Ireland, if you built a house on a fairy path, misfortune would prevail, and it was believed that only by moving the house would the misfortune stop. Brick houses that were built ignoring warnings that they could have an effect on the spirits would suffer dire outcomes. These houses could be destroyed by storms, yet mysteriously leaving a wooden building next to them still standing.

Also, in folklore there are ghost paths (which seem to start or end at a cemetery) where the dead body would be driven along what was called a 'dead man's road'. This allowed the spirit of the deceased to thrive.

There have been certain curious funeral customs throughout history that must also be adhered to, such as having to put down the coffin at a crossroads, or the need to walk around the church three times on the way to the grave.

These tales and many more exist all over the world, but where would such ideas come from if people didn't realise there are certain forces at work here?

Some people might wonder why it's important to remember these facts as they are from so long ago, but I believe we should, as we can learn a lot about tradition and why people tended to give such notions the time of day.

However, religion has changed a lot of our history, by changing stories such as 'The Fairy Doorway' into 'The doorways leading to the Devil' just to keep people away. Yet, ironically, it is also where you will probably find a religious cross to 'own' the site.

It's said that these standing stones vibrate or sing, and this singing can intensify at certain times of the year, such as before and after the winter solstice, and tests have been carried out on the radioactivity using a Geiger counter to measure the radiation and to prove the fact that this energy is all around us. How can so many people find it hard to accept that this energy does affect us? After all, we see birds and animals leaving an area before disasters occur.

'Lose your mind and come to your senses.' Fritz Perls, German Psychiatrist and Psychotherapist

I suppose many people have just lost the ability to feel/see or hear certain frequencies, as it isn't taught at school. It's not surprising that 'clear seeing' has been made out to be bad, as it's a very powerful tool. Thousands of years ago, a priest or shaman would have made the connection for us and communed with spirit ancestors for guidance. The same behaviour a hundred years ago would have been called witchcraft, or even schizophrenia. I suppose it's a fine line between those who make a living from talking to people who aren't there and those who are locked up for a similar thing.

However, many people today are waking up to feeling or reading the energy of a place. I now believe that if more people learn how to tune into their bodies and their environment, the need to call in an outside 'body' to 'cleanse' a building/area would not be necessary, as the pineal gland in the head can give us changes in our consciousness when the magnetic and radioactive effects of the earth change.

When this centre is activated and worked with, we 'see' more clearly, enabling us to know intuitively when something is okay for us or not. It's important that we find out what kind of energy is around us in the places we live and work, as if we have any of these stress lines in our home or workplace, it can affect us in all kinds of ways.

You can use a pendulum or dowsing rods to see the energy around you.

It's great to see how the rods cross over as you walk into the energy field. Dowsing rods have been in use for a very long time to look for water, etc., so don't be worried about thinking that it is part of the occult (although the word occult simply means the unknown).

Some people feel that the effect of 'energy work' is purely psychological and due to suggestion, but you cannot influence the behaviour of animals and plants, and most animals will seek a good place to sleep and can become ill if forced to sleep in a position that has Geopathic Stress. Plants and trees often have stunted growth in GS places, and there have been cases where babies have moved all over the cot/bed trying to avoid GS in their sleep.

Also, sometimes, stress can be left by a previous occupant of a building or can even be there before the building was erected, as energy doesn't die, it only transforms.

In more serious cases we could even feel the chilling presence of the 'memory' of a brutal attack or murder, which would imprint and stay in the area so that as people passed through this space, they would feel a 'chill'.

For those who are finely tuned to energy (sensitives), they could tap into this memory and be able to pick up certain emotions or feelings that would link to the event, just as we see with certain TV programmes showing such subjects.

> 'Science without religion is lame, religion without science is blind.'
> Albert Einstein

One of the best pieces of evidence I found was when I first looked into crystals. I needed answers for how crystals had helped ease my back pain, as well as my sleeping habits. I'd started reading up on the subject and the book I was reading informed me that crystals were great for helping plants.

I had a plant that was at death's door and had been so for a long time (I should have thrown it away, but I was hanging on to it for sentimental reasons). So, I got out of bed, went downstairs to find the few crystals that I had and placed them around the plant.

Feeling very silly about my actions (I was very sceptical at this time) I went back to bed, deciding that I would throw the stones and the book away the next morning as my behaviour had gone far enough. However, when I went down the next morning I couldn't believe my eyes. It wasn't possible! The plant actually had buds starting to form on the branches (and no, I hadn't watered it – it had been under the stairs for weeks). I really thought I'd lost the plot, as did my family and friends when I showed them the plant, and I asked myself many times how this could have happened. Could it have happened simply to get me on my journey into this subject?

I now know that the most important thing is it doesn't really matter. However, my searching has always brought more questions than answers and I'm comfortable with that now, as perhaps we're just not meant to know everything. A little mystery can be a wonderful thing.

I found that the more I studied the subject of energy, the more I came across experiences that took me further into the subject. Not only was I finding out how my environment affected my life, but, in turn, how it affected those I came into contact with. These experiences made me realise I was picking up emotions too, and later, I started to pick up the energy of places.

One morning, I was sat chatting to my friend in a café in India and a man drove up on a moped. I glanced at him, but other than that I took no notice until he sat in the seat behind me. Instantly, I had to get up and run next door to the pub toilet. I closed the door and felt so weird!

I burst into tears, and as I covered my face with my hands, in my mind's eye I saw the most awful images. I felt like I was in hell! I didn't know what was going on or why this was happening to me. These images were horrendous, with people wailing and clawing to get out from 'somewhere'.

Eventually, I came out from the toilet and, as I walked back to my friend, I beckoned her to come and sit outside with me. I tried to tell her what had just happened and apologised for running out and leaving her. I said that there was something about the man that had sat down behind me. I was trying to describe what I had just been through and told her the nearest description I could give was from a horror movie, where you see lost souls all clawing to get out of hell.

> '*If you are going through hell ... keep going.*'
> Winston Churchill

Feeling really odd and thinking my friend would want to have me certified (she was a mental nurse), she actually surprised me by saying that what I was describing was probably the mental state the man was in, as she knew he was a heroin user. She went on to tell me that I'd picked up a good description of where he probably was mentally. I was amazed that she even believed me!

Learning about energy became intriguing, but during my learning the shop became a nightmare, with illness, moods, cold spots, etc. They all took their toll on my thoughts and emotions, as well as my body. It started affecting other people, too. I was begged by those around me to leave the building before 'it's too late', as they witnessed some freaky goings-on. I eventually found sense and moved to the seaside for six months, and my health started to change for the better.

Then, without showing any respect for what I'd learnt from the shop experience, I moved back to my hometown and straight into a place that had the exact energy I'd had in the shop. Within a week of moving in, I had a really bad 'accident' and fractured my back, as well as straining all the ligaments and tendons in my left foot.

I kept asking 'them upstairs' why this was happening and what I could possibly be learning from all this chaos. Then it came to me that I should be working on writing about the energy we live with daily. When I had my shops, customers would often come in and ask for help with 'hauntings' or 'bad luck'. I would give them as much help and advice as possible, yet I always believed it's better for them to have the power by learning about what was troubling their home/life.

Although I'd come across the subject of energy after a long series of illnesses, I still chose to carry on pretending it didn't exist, or I would allow others to mock my beliefs. Yet, I knew that if I spent a long time on my mobile or on a Wi-Fi computer, my symptoms would reoccur. My head would buzz, which the doctors put down to tinnitus. I kept trying to say the buzzing was not in my ears, it was in the top of my head. As usual, I waited for another problem with my body to become severe before I decided to look back at the work I'd researched over the years.

> '*Man can learn nothing except by going from the known to the unknown.*' – Claude Bernard

When I began researching the subject, I was told about a man called Rolf Gordon who'd written a book called *Geopathic Stress* after years of his own research on the subject. Mr Gordon had lost his son to cancer before he looked into this subject and I waited until my body was very low before I went back to what I already knew: *Geopathic Stress hurts the body*.

Rolf states that there are thousands of doctors worldwide that recognise the seriousness of GS, and we must deal with this before we can heal 100%, as the body will not repair itself when it is bombarded with a low volt energy system.

How could I know this and choose to ignore it?

On a recent trip to India, I met a lady who actually started telling me that she suffers from sensitivity to Wi-Fi and mobiles. I actually thought she must have heard about my problem, but she hadn't. In fact, she was relieved when I told her I shared the same problem. I felt like she'd given me gold! To find someone who actually understood my issues was the biggest relief, especially when she described the same symptoms. She is so sensitive to this energy that she knows if a Wi-Fi computer is on in a certain part of the building.

There are many sites about GS on the Internet, so surely we can't ignore it now. How many more of us are going to be ill or even die before we see that the body is like a sponge and that we soak up this energy? GS has been linked to conditions like ME, cancer, asthma and heart problems, and some say even cot death. It's also linked to rage (including child abuse), allergy to foods and hyperactive behaviour.

During sleep your brain is supposed to rest half the time and is busy healing your body the other half. However, if you are geopathically stressed during sleep your brain has to spend all of its time working due to the strain of GS and you wake up tired, and as the GS of the earth seems to be much stronger at night, it's obvious that this is also when we are our most vulnerable to it.

Sleep is very important, and a long time ago we would sleep on the earth to charge our bodies. Sleep is also used to create new cells, giving the right signals for the body to absorb the correct levels of vitamins and minerals and also to adjust the hormones. GS can interfere with this and leave the immune system weak.

Also, when we don't feel well we go to bed, but if your bed is in a place that has GS you are making the matter worse. GS doesn't actually cause illness, but it lowers the immune system and the ability to fight off viruses and bacteria. That's why most people who work with Feng Shui realise that GS is the first thing to check for to ensure a 'happy home'.

Check out Rolf's website for diagrams on where to place beds, etc. and for other information, as it includes the fact that cars, hospitals, etc. are all affected. It's said to have been proven to the satisfaction of the medical profession over 70 years ago that GS is detrimental to human health, yet in this country we feel silly trying to get it recognised.

Some indications of GS can be feeling rundown, tired, nervous or depressed and sleeplessness, when you finally get to sleep having bad dreams, when you wake having a fuzzy head, and children can also wet the bed or babies can cry constantly. Tingling in the arms or feeling really cold are other symptoms (we certainly had really extreme cold spots in my second shop).

People that can't shake off an illness or depression, or simply just feel below par all the time, can ask some simple questions to see if they could be suffering from this problem, like:

'Did the problem start after I moved into the new building?' or

'Do I feel better when I am away from the place I work?' and can try to find out if the previous people who lived or worked there also suffered.

You can also check if the premises were built on an old water vein. I found out that my old house had been built on an area that had naturally been a stream and they had moved it to build the housing estate, but over time it was shifting back. Also, a place that's unnaturally cold or damp could be a good indication that it needs checking.

Quoted from Rolf's website:

'*Research has shown Geopathic Stress is mainly caused by narrow paths of running water about 200 to 300 ft below ground. This creates an electromagnetic field, which disturbs the earth's natural vibrations, in particular, the beneficially 7.83 Hz (cycle per second) Alpha vibrations (confirmed by NASA). The Alpha vibrations can be as high as 250 Hz in very Geopathic Stressed people. The USA scientist George Lakowsky confirmed in the '30s that humans (and animals) have less chance of fighting bacteria and viruses at higher than normal vibrations.*

'*The effect GS has on the human body has been most convincingly proved by a major research project undertaken by the University of Vienna direct by Professor Dr Otto Berman. In order to eliminate any placebo effect the tests were organized in a double-blind fashion. Neither examining doctors nor the people tested knew whether they had been sitting in a GS place or neutral place. 985 people were tested and subjected to a very thorough medical examination before and after tests. Tests included blood sedimentation, electric condulance of certain muscle points, blood pressure, heartbeat, breathing, skin resistance and blood circulation. The people tested only sat in a GS or neutral place for 15 minutes. The harmful effect could be registered in most of the people who sat in a GS place. 'One can imagine the consequences which exposure to Geopathic Stress over many years could have,' wrote Natural Medicine.*

'We have hardly come across anybody who has died of meningitis, E. Coli food poisoning, BSE, Legionnaires Disease and SARS without being GS.

'The UK has over 800 earthquakes and 20,000 landslides each year, which can affect GS. Nearby roads and building works can also alter the GS in your home. So check your home and bed positions once a year. Fortunately, a 'good' home will seldom suddenly become a 'bad' home and some homes get better. During the night, at full moon or winter and stormy weather, GS is always stronger.'

It is claimed that Queen Victoria sent dowsers to Scotland to find the 'good energy' area and they came up with where Balmoral now stands. Further research shows that most castles and places of royalty have very little GS.

Thankfully, when I had my problem with the shop a very clever man called Jeff Moran came in to do one of his Sound Workshops, and as it happened I wasn't there when he arrived. My friend welcomed him in and the first thing he said to her was,

'The energy in here is really weird.'

She looked at him, knowing that neither of us had told anyone about the problems we were facing, and wondered how he knew. He then set about saying he had to check it out before he could begin working.

After only a few minutes, he told her we had a huge GS line running straight through the shop and into the back room (where people had reported a 'spinning' sensation during therapy). He made some alterations and placed crystals in certain positions, which helped.

It's said that GS can have a severe psychological effect on people and may be present in cases where people are suicidal, and is also another suggestion why people get divorced. The good news is there are thousands of doctors worldwide that recognise the seriousness of GS and know that we must deal with it. In most cases the problem can be sorted once it is recognised, as the body returns to free-flowing energy and good health once the GS has been cleared out of the system. Remember, GS doesn't actually cause the illness, it weakens the immune system, which stops your chance of fighting any bacteria or virus.

Electromagnetic Fields

Electromagnetic fields (EMFs) from power lines are recognised by IARC (the International Agency for Research in Cancer) as a possible carcinogen in light of the persistent association with childhood leukaemia. Apart from

EMFs, power lines emit corona ions, causing clouds of charged aerosol particles to drift in the wind, although it has not been firmly established that this causes specific harm.

Stress-sensitive hormones have been found to be elevated in people at work in electromagnetic environments (and in EHS sufferers), but not when they are at leisure. I certainly know this to be the case when I'm in another country.

Countries like Sweden are taking this matter very seriously and have already adopted precautionary measures for these problems; many doctors actually treat these conditions, as well as offer advice on how to avoid such problems, including painting walls with a special paint that can stop the radiation coming into the homes of people living near phone masts.

Here in my own area people living near such equipment are fighting to get recognition of the link between the electrical pylons and the high percentage of cancer. More than 23,000 homes in Britain are near power lines, as well as many offices, schools and other premises.

Electrohypersensitivity (EHS) is an officially fully recognised functional impairment in Sweden (it's not regarded as a disease). The person is met in a respectful way, with all the necessary support, with the goal being to eliminate the impairment. Yet, I find myself feeling embarrassed when I try to explain that I believe it adds to my tiredness, etc.

Electromagnetic fields surround us, it's a fact, and they are hundreds of millions of times stronger than natural background levels. We've not had time to adapt to the radiation from our use of electricity, mobiles, cordless phones and other wireless devices, resulting in problems such as:

∗ Sleep problems – inability to get a 'good' night's sleep, waking up and restlessness

∗ Abnormal tiredness, weakness, tremors, faintness and dizziness

∗ Headaches – sometimes extremely severe

∗ Tinnitus and earaches

∗ Skin feels dry, prone to rashes, irritation, skin tingling, crawling sensation

∗ Chest pains, heart arrhythmias

∗ Warmth or burning on face, not unlike strong sunburn

∗ Pain in teeth and jaws

∗ Eyes – difficulty in seeing, smarting, irritating sensation, pain or a gritty feeling

* Aches, pain, prickling sensations in joints and muscles
Cognitive
* Memory – short-term and long-term memory impairment
* Lack of concentration
* Difficulty in learning new things
Emotional
* Depression, mood changes, including anger and crying
* Irritability
* Stress and anxiety attacks, feeling out of control.

Studies have found that children whose birth address was within 200 metres of an overhead power line had a 70% increased risk of having leukaemia, and those living 200 to 600 metres away from power lines had a 20% increased risk. Worse still, the study had been partially funded by the power line industry!

In the June 2005 British Medical Journal, a study concludes that there is a statistical link between EMF from power lines and leukaemia. The study, a collaboration between the Childhood Cancer Research Group at the University of Oxford and National Grid owners Transco, looked at cancer data of children up to the age of fifteen in England and Wales between 1962 and 1995.

However, the issue is still classed as 'open' by EMF specialists in respect of EMF and cancer. Anyone interested in looking at this subject further can simply type into the search engine 'power lines and cancer'. I found a lot of helpful and alarming information, including something called 'Revolt' covering my local area.

CHAPTER 8

Orbs and Ghosts

ORBS HAVE BECOME a fascination for me since I visited the Elephanta Caves in Mumbai, India. I'd been taking pictures of the fantastic statues of Shiva, Kali and Buddha, and when I returned to the hotel room and looked at my camera, to my amazement they were there!

Some of the orbs (or balls of light) were pure white, while others were multicoloured and one was bright yellow. I was stunned! I checked my camera – it seemed okay – and then I took more photos to see if they showed up again, but the pictures were normal. I thought about the orbs all night, as I hadn't seen anything like it before.

The strange thing is that I've seen them ever since, in many different countries and with different cameras. It's said that some orbs can be produced by accident due to the elements around at the time, such as humidity, dust or airborne particles. So don't take every picture that has a round speck on it as having one.

For me, they seem to fall into two groups. One is a solid colour and the other always has a black 'centre'. These seem to be made up of many colours. I wonder if the ones with a centre are 'alive', as we are made of a core and have all the colours of the rainbow in our energy field.

I know the sceptics say that it is only dust moving as the picture is taken, but that doesn't explain the ones that move very slowly across the shot of a video. It's also said that my photos are a reflection of a surface, but I have ones that are taken with no surface that could cause a reflection. More importantly, last year I actually saw an orb with my own eyes as I was taking the picture.

Many believe that orbs are ghosts in the form of balls of light (as some seem to have a 'face' in them). They are believed to be the human soul or life force of those that once inhabited a physical body here on earth. Ghost hunters encounter them quite frequently and, to date, many have actually photographed them. I even heard Noel Edmunds admit that he has thousands of pictures of orbs.

Some experts say they are spirits that have stayed close to earth, as they feel bound to their previous life or location. I seem to capture them at family gatherings and wonder if it's our deceased relatives wanting to enjoy the party.

They can appear transparent or display themselves in a bright solid form, and I've been told that it's not hard to capture them on film in the circular form since the spirit may choose a ball of light, as this takes less energy than showing up in a 'human' guise (ghost).

One of the strangest photos I own is of me and a friend in India, taken with my digital camera. When we looked at it, a misty figure was at my left side. Another friend had taken a photo of us at the same time on an ordinary old film camera, and when she had it developed, the exact same shape showed up.

It's also said that ghosts and orbs find it easier to show themselves in the colder parts of the year, as that's when there is the most static electricity in the atmosphere. But even people who believe in the paranormal can't agree which is which, and rightly so. We should always believe what WE believe, not what others tell us.

So you make up your own mind as to what they are when you come across them. For anyone interested in finding out more about these fascinating little mysteries, there is a lot of information around, especially on the web, and if you would like to view my pictures, go to www.thenergywithin.co.uk

Ghosts

Once again, this subject brings up much debate and I believe it's only when you experience a ghost or spirit that you will know whether or not they're real. Many believe that ghosts and spirits are not the same thing and, as with many subjects not of the 'norm', we find many different ideas and beliefs about who is right.

As always, I can only write what I believe to be true and my intention is to open the door to something that is very much part of our existence here on earth. Even people who have experienced spirits seem to fall into two groups. One believes they are a physical manifestation and the other believes they are in the mind of the person who had the experience. Neither seems to be able to prove they are right.

Then there are the many accounts of people experiencing the same thing at the same time, as well as those who have religious sightings in large groups, such as seeing the Virgin Mary, Bernadette at Lourdes or the children of Fatima.

I know some believe that if a person has seen a loved one at the foot of the bed it could be wishful thinking or purely a result of grief, but that can't explain my experience, as I didn't know the man I saw in my bedroom. Well, not when I saw him anyway, but you can read the full intriguing story in my forthcoming book *Till the End of Midnight*.

There are also cases of a sighting of someone when the person hasn't actually died yet! Then I remembered a situation in my shop, where a customer asked me who the girl was that she'd seen standing in the corner looking at the crystals. I had to tell her that she'd been the only customer in the shop for the last hour. It's fascinating, this subject of energy!

I also remember when I was in hospital many years ago and a lady opposite me had to be moved to a room on her own, as her health had deteriorated. She knew I believed in the afterlife and asked me to pray for her. I did more than that! I asked for my spirit guide to help her and sit with her, as I knew she was afraid. Then I went to sleep.

A couple of days later she came to my bed and thanked me for sending 'the man'. I was really surprised, as even though I'd asked I didn't really expect it to happen. She went on to describe his appearance and the time he came to her – precisely when I'd asked! Years later she was at a party I was attending, and told everyone about that night and how I'd sent her an angel.

> '*The most beautiful thing we can experience is the mysterious. It is the source of all true art and all science.*' Albert Einstein, Theoretical Physicist

Some say that spirits come to give us help and others come because they need our help, maybe to pass over to another dimension if they're earthbound. If you experience what you consider to be a spirit in your life, you should consider all the reasons for what is happening first, as it could be the location where you are living. You must consider your lifestyle too, as certain activities that you're involved in might be drawing certain events to you.

Certain conditions such as emotional problems often draw the unpleasant experience of a poltergeist to the home, especially if there are children approaching their teens. It's believed to be their energy becoming so potent that creates these experiences. If they have emotional problems too, it's a very strong energy to have.

Children are supposed to be more able to see spirits than adults, due to the fact that they are more open minded and haven't closed the 'doorway'. That is, until others tell them that spirits, etc. don't exist.

I've had many experiences with spirit activity in one form or another, but once I learnt more about the subject, I realised that a lot of my problems were linked with what was going on in my life at the time. I remember not having much choice of where to go for help when a spirit was terrifying us in our home. Thankfully, things have changed a great deal, although care is needed when looking for help, as I believe that not all people are genuine.

We've had many films showing us that ghosts have seriously disrupted the lives of some people, or that they play pranks and move things about. In some cases it's even glamorised to dabble in such worlds, but in my opinion things such as Ouija boards and other similar devices should be avoided!

It isn't that the board itself is the danger, it's the fact that you are allowing yourself to use something that can lower your own will. You are handing over the car keys, so to speak. Yet, if we were taught about this kind of subject, we would be more armed to do something about it.

That brings us to the question: does the person who sees the spirit bring it from their subconscious, or does the spirit form some kind of telepathy with the person who sees it? If the latter is the case, how could the seer receive the information in cases where a spirit perhaps had his face blown off in the war? Or in the case where a spirit is dressed in a certain attire, why choose to appear in that way?

> '_To believe in the things you can see and can touch is no belief at all, but to believe in the unseen is both a triumph and a blessing._'
> Bob Proctor, Author and Lecturer

If we accept it has a consciousness, then we can believe that the personality of the spirit can then make the decision to appear how and to whom it likes. For me, the idea of it having a consciousness makes more sense, as I remember doing a 'reading' for a lady and describing her gran to her in great detail.

However, she looked rather puzzled as I gave her information from her gran. When I asked her why she was looking at me that way, she informed me that everything I had told her was correct, except for one problem, her Gran WAS STILL ALIVE!

My immediate thought was that she'd died that day without the lady knowing, but then more information came through and I saw her gran sitting in an armchair in a nursing home.

I asked the lady if her gran suffered from dementia, and she confirmed that was correct. Wow, I thought! This is amazing! I'd never been taught this could happen. Her gran was slipping in and out of this world and I had caught her on one of her travels.

As if that's not mind-boggling enough, just think of the way we create the images in dreams or meditating, when we visualise and experience with so much detail, or in the case of Past Life Regression, where we actually FEEL the things too.

When we try to fit these subjects into boxes we hit a brick wall, as there are so many cases that can be argued against. Therefore, I have concluded that there are more things to heaven and earth, and maybe we don't always need to have an answer for everything.

Some people live with spirits without any problem, and they don't seem to mind as long as the spirit doesn't bother them; others live with them without having a clue they are there. Many companies are around now that 'clear' homes of unwanted spirits, but in some cases, after asking the spirit to leave it returns, as it simply doesn't want to go.

If you do find yourself in this situation and have a problem spirit, read whatever responsible, reliable book you can, but remember not to work through fear, or you might be misled. Spirits can be mischievous, but they are usually only trying to let you know they are there. They probably want you to know for a specific reason, such as because a birthday or an anniversary is due, or they may be trying to comfort you if you're having a hard time. After all, these people would do the same if they were still alive, and just because a person has left the physical body doesn't mean they have stopped caring.

Mind you, I remember one case when a friend was called into a house that had become 'active' after they had decorated (this shifts the energy and disturbs it) and moved the furniture too. They'd put the TV cabinet in another part of the room, and when the medium got there she discovered that the 'lady' (spirit) was angry, as that's where she had laid her baby and the TV was interfering with it (vibrationally).

A lot of people believe it's their imagination when they see a spirit, as they have caught it in the corner of their eye and when they turn around its gone. This is due to the brain; when you are not focusing it registers with the left side, and then when you turn your head round the right side of your brain takes over and the spirit is no longer there.

Another question always asked is why are they always seen at night? Well, at night there's less electricity in the building, which can interfere, and also they are easier to see in the dark. After all, they are made up of energy. As energy isn't solid, they also seem to be able to change their vibration to that of a wall, etc. They can then blend with that energy and move through it. We may think it's impossible, but the laws of physics say differently.

A sign of a house having a spirit can be something like footsteps, knocks or bangs; don't forget to do the obvious and check it isn't something that can be explained, as our imagination can run wild in these situations, especially when we are filled with fear. Plus, if it's not a nice spirit, it will actually feed off your fear.

The thing to remember is that if you have a bad spirit (although I don't like using the word bad) in a building, trust me, you'll know the difference between that and your gran trying to let you know she's there.

The problem is we've been fed horror films and it's easy to get the two mixed up. That's another reason why I believe we should be taught about phenomena in school, as the more we know about something, the better we are at dealing with such things. Empowerment has to be the key.

It can be a minefield wondering how to learn about this subject, but if you are responsible and use your gut feeling you will be drawn to the best group or class for you, as we all get what we need when we need it.

The secret is trusting in yourself that you are having the experiences that you need at that time. Yes, even a 'haunting', as without seeing my first spirit I probably wouldn't have spent the last ten years doing what I have been doing.

> '*Socrates, you will remember, asked all the important questions, but he never answered any of them.*' Dickinson Edwards

Today, a lot of people are picking up energy in general, including spirits, smells or sounds, and again, I ask you to refer to the chapter on chakras, as this will give you the basic information to decide where to go next, and whether you want to go further. Being of service can be an enjoyment, but I must stress the subject of personal responsibility.

Animals are great at picking up on a spirit, but as usual, check it's not a fly, a light or something similar that the dog or cat has seen. I was left in no doubt with one of my cats, as he would sit for ages staring at a corner of the room and tilt his head as if someone was talking to him. He did this so often that eventually, we became used to it.

However, it was a different situation when we had a nasty 'visitor', as our hi-fi would get turned off, or a record or tape would be stopped halfway through the song. And one night, when it became too much, I had to bring all the children into my bedroom because I feared for our safety, as the loud bangs we heard became so loud that it felt as if they were coming from within the walls.

Lights are another thing that freaks people out, as their electrical equipment goes bananas. Once again, realise that a spirit is made of energy just like the electrics, so what better way to attract attention?

Some people have the awful experience of being 'touched' by a spirit. A few years ago I was asked to go to a pub where the landlord had been having problems with the dog being spooked and things getting moved, but it was only when he was 'touched' that we were called in to investigate.

If you have a problem with banging or closing doors, ask someone else to look at the situation, as they may be able to see it with a different eye. A plumber or carpenter could solve your problem before you look up the local ghostbusters.

However, if they can't sort it for you and you do need help, try your local spiritualist church. If nothing else, they will offer you advice and support – they certainly did with me.

Some people say they don't mind the spirit being in their home, but they're not pets and they have somewhere else that would be better for their growth. So as much as it's a great way to entertain guests or it may help in getting customers into a pub, it's best all round if you at least suggest to them that they don't belong there. Of course, it is their choice to stay or go, but at least you're giving them a choice.

A 'passing' is a very painful time for us and as we're not educated in dealing and accepting death, we sometimes sit at a bedside and ask or even beg the person not to leave us, and as they love us, they will often oblige. However, it's a natural part of the journey of life and should be aided, not hindered.

I've had the privilege to be part of two passings in my family and, although difficult emotionally, I knew it was best for them to leave, as they were in so much pain. I think to be witness to someone entering and leaving this world is such a privilege, although needless to say, emotionally, birth was the more popular.

Indigenous people looked on this so differently, as they used to welcome death and help the person in any way they could. One of the most intriguing things I learnt was that in the Aborigine tribal culture, the person ready to leave would tell the others they wanted to go 'back home', so they would organise a party to gather everyone and celebrate the life of the one leaving.

After they had discussed all the things the person had done, and they'd eaten and danced, the person 'going' would then lie down and remove his energy from his physical body while the others witnessed it, being happy for the one going back home to spirit. Then they would leave the person's body and walk away, taking any personal belongings with them. The body would be left for the animals to take what they wanted, as they had been kind enough to give their bodies to the human when they needed it. What a recycling system they had!

Many of the ancient cultures believed in the afterlife, including the Egyptians, who believed they had a 'ka', which is an exact copy of the physical body, and that we have a 'ba' (soul). When we die, the ka is left with provisions for the afterlife so it doesn't have to go around bothering the living, while the ba goes to the next world (similar to Irish traditions).

> '*Truth is like the stars: it shows only in the darkness of the night.*'
> The Eye of the Prophet, Khalil Gibran

I have encountered a few experiences with the paranormal and not all nice, I must say, but one of the most frightening was when I was in bed and was overtaken by what I can only call 'the blackness'. It was like being in a completely darkened room. Then I was 'picked up' and shaken for what seemed like ages, but I suppose it could only have been minutes.

I screamed for my son to come in, but as I was shouting the sound was going nowhere. There was nothing but silence. It was the strangest experience! Of course afterwards, I was pleased that my son hadn't heard me, but at the time he was the only one I could think of to help me. Needless to say, when it stopped I put the light on and it stayed on for the rest of the night.

Christianity doesn't allow for the existence of ghosts because of fear-based doctrines, but how come they have information on performing exorcism? They teach us about heaven, hell and purgatory (where they say departed souls go) yet do not teach how to deal with such things.

Yet, Christ taught us that we could do what he could, and more.

Some great names over the years have believed in spiritualism, including Edgar Alan Poe, Houdini and the Royal family. The Society for Psychic Research was founded as far back as 1882, although the belief in the afterlife goes back way before then, as many of the ancient cultures buried their dead with food, etc. to help them in the next world, and many steps were taken to try to keep them there so they didn't come back.

So the answer to the question are ghosts real, is yes, they are. But then I would say that, wouldn't I? After all, it's how I met my father, fifteen years after he died.

When we cross over to the other side of life that we call death, we leave our attachment with the physical world by leaving the vehicle that keeps us here. The soul or spirit body separates from the physical body. Death is just a rearrangement of the elements, all going back to what they were, ENERGY.

But we have stored images of death in our psyche. We fear death because we don't want to fade away. We fear that all we once were will be lost, but this is our past and that should be let go of anyway.

If we could 'die' every moment we could discover everlasting life, but we need our view of the subject to change dramatically first.

Death isn't the opposite of life, it is a part of it.

Life is all about change.

Stagnation is the opposite of life.

Die every day and we have a new life every day.

It's what we do with that day that's important.

CHAPTER 9

Metaphysics

WHEN WE EXAMINE the word Metaphysics, it is essentially two words: Meta and Physics. Meta means change, like metamorphosis, or after, higher, beyond, as in metaphysics. Physics is the science dealing with the properties and relationship between matter and energy in the known universe. So when we speak of metaphysics, we are talking about things beyond matter and energy.

What did the ancients know that we don't?

Well, they certainly seemed to be able to connect with the force of nature. They must have had the knowledge that we are not separate, as the language they used reflected this. The word enthused comes from the Greek word Entheos and means 'the God within'; surely that tells us something. By doing something with enthusiasm we are doing it with our full, true power (from the solar plexus), which is also where our will is situated. If we try to do something that is not from our full power, or our best intention, then the project will not be completed at its best.

And as everything is energy in motion (e-motion), the energy we put into a job is reflected and will be imprinted into the object concerned, i.e. if we cook a meal in a bad mood, it will not be as good as when we cook in a good mood. Ironing a shirt in a bad mood will also have an effect on the person wearing it. I have seen evidence of this with dream catchers, when they've been made in a sweatshop factory instead of with the best intention. That's another word to watch for, in-tension. It means to have your power ready for what you've focused on. So, if an intention is set, it has a better chance of hitting the desired target. If not, it could go anywhere and to anyone, and this is often why many dreams are shattered.

11.11

One of most intriguing subjects I came across in my learning was the

11.11 phenomena. It has been said that 11.11 = spiritual awakening. It's like a Guardian Angel, a doorway or spiritual portal and since coming across this subject I have noticed it more and more.

I may be working on the computer and I'll notice the time is 11.11, or I'll randomly glance at a clock to find it will be 11.11; and my friends are noticing it, too. It's said to be a link to the intelligence trying to help us through the next stage of evolution, as the 11.11 enigma has been here for a while now and has affected the lives of countless thousands of people.

For many people, seeing the 11s in such abundance makes them certain that this goes far beyond the realms of coincidence, and can be seen as a crack between two worlds or as a bridge to an entirely different spiral of evolution.

I have been seeing the 11.11 number combinations everywhere for about six years and at first I put it down to coincidence. Without going too deep into the subject, one and one is also the beginning of the Fibonacci curve, which is the universal pattern of nature found in everything from conch shells to galaxy spirals.

And if you times 1111 by 1111 you get 1234321, representing a pyramid of which the number 11 is a sacred number, with the proportions of the great pyramid being the ratio 7:11. The number 11 is also a number harmonious with Pi, and therefore, it seems that it is also a very important number when you understand the mathematical infrastructure of the universe.

Some say that 11.11 is a pre-encoded trigger placed into our cellular memory banks prior to our descent into matter, which when activated signifies that our time of completion is near. This refers to the completion of duality. When 11.11 appears to you, it could be your wake-up call, as it's a time for reflection.

In numerology the three 'master' numbers of 11, 22 and 33 are considered special, as they magnify the energy of a single digit number. The number 11 is the most intuitive of numbers as it represents illumination (numbers are calculated to a single digit except master numbers), and what really blew me away was the information on the Mayan calendar.

Many of us have wondered why it ends in 2012, which to many refers to the end of the world, although many in the new way of thinking actually believe it's only the end of the old way of thinking.

Not only does the calendar end in 2012, it ends on the equinox on 21 December 2012. Add this up and it comes to 11. If that isn't mind-blowing enough, the winter solstice on that date is at exactly 11.11 a.m.

This is said to be the emergence of a utopian world, a bridge between duality and oneness, which is the next stage of our evolution and has been spoken of for a long time by people such as the Maya, Aztec and the Hopi Indians, who tell of a series of worlds or cycles of civilisation.

This process of synchronisation with our own intuition and the universe is about learning to live in harmony with nature and its time cycles, as many of us now know that the original calendar had 13 months, not 12. This awakening of our conscious awareness to the synchronicities and the natural order of life can be done by choosing to follow the original calendar that's based on the harmonic mathematics of the Ancient Maya, which was purposely designed as a solar-lunar-galactic calendar for the modern world to reconnect with the sacred essence of time.

In light of the 2012 prophecy, people around the world are being guided to choose to synchronise with this life-changing tool, and as we have a web of communication in the Internet, it's easier to allow others access to this important information. The downside to that is that we also have more access to the endless fear and panic that is shown, but we must see past that and realise that WE are creating this world, therefore WE must make sure we play our part in it!

> '*There are two ways to be fooled. One is to believe what isn't true; the other is to refuse to believe what is true.*' Soren Kierkegaard, Danish Philosopher and Theologian

A common aspect from the Hopi is that we are currently in the fourth world, as the third world ended with a 'cleansing' by a great flood, just as the Bible mentions. In fact, similar traditions of a worldwide catastrophe exist among people of all continents, including the Greeks, Egyptians, Hebrews, Persians, Hindus and native North and South Americans. Many tribes and cultures also foresaw what was about to happen.

Native American leaders told of a man that would have a forked tongue and would speak of many good things by which they would be tempted. They told of force being used in an attempt to trap them into using weapons, and that if they did, they would be brought to their knees.

Teachings and prophecies informed them to be alert for the signs and omens that would come to give courage and strength. They were told of earthquakes and floods that would cause great disasters, changing the seasons and bringing about the disappearance of certain wildlife. They said this was the Universal Plan, which the Great Spirit has spoken of since the dawn of time.

They also knew of a gradual corruption and confusion among world leaders and wars sweeping across the globe, and said that when this happened we would know their prophecies were coming true. I suppose most of us can say we are witnessing this now.

I found it interesting that they also mentioned men bringing back pieces of the moon, which will upset the balance and unleash disastrous forces. My grandmother always insisted that the world and the weather would never be the same after the first rocket was launched into space. I laughed at the time, thinking she was just being old fashioned, but I have quoted her on many occasions over the past thirty years.

Thankfully, they also told of the ills of the earth being cured and that Mother Earth would bloom once again, with all the people uniting in peace and harmony for a very long time to come. They also said the 'purification' would begin shortly after humans built a great house in the sky (space stations).

I was thrilled when I fulfilled my dream to go to New Mexico and meet with Hopi Indians after a meditation had shown me my guide. I didn't know at the time that, when he drew a symbol for me in the sand (in the meditation), the meaning of the message was from the Hopi tribe, and I later bought a necklace from a shop in Albuquerque on which was the symbol. They have an energy that is hard to describe and the memory of watching the 'Gathering of the Nations' will stay with me for the rest of my life.

The Future

Rather than preparing for some future moment down the road, let's notice how we are living life in this moment. We need to wake up and realise that we're already in the midst of a planetary transformation process and we all have a unique role to play here. We need to follow our inspiration, to find our passion and to feel alive.

That's why following fear thoughts doesn't serve us, because the voices of self-doubt and anxiety don't inspire us to be part of the solution; rather they clog us up and often lead us to shut down from our positive creativity.

'*We cannot solve our problems with the same thinking we used when we created them.*' Albert Einstein

We can help make the transition period for our world a little easier by learning all we can about our part in it all. That's right, OUR part in it, as information is available about how we can become more responsible, and more spiritual instead of material. I'm not saying we don't deserve a good life with luxuries, I'm saying that we all deserve that.

Living in the moment simply means bringing heaven down to earth and creating what we want our life to be like. It means ridding ourselves of martyrdom and being the victim, understanding how our energy works and makes us who we are, and letting our energy flow in harmony with the universe. Once we learn how to do that, we can go with the flow; we'll always be in the right place at the right time, allowing miracles to happen.

We won't need to struggle when things begin to go wrong in life, as we'll recognise that we're not in flow. It's about living from the heart and trusting in the self instead of others, whether it's a partner, boss, our parents or religion.

It's about taking FULL responsibility for our daily life and having the courage to change things when we're not happy, and having confidence in our SELF and the universe (whatever you term that to be) to make the necessary changes. Understanding this new dimension can bring us much joy in life.

We'll realise that we can change our life and anything that's making us unhappy, and that WE have whatever it takes to change the situation, if we set our intention of what we want moment by moment, knowing that whatever's happening to us is our responsibility; notice the word I use is responsibility, not blame or fault.

Response-ability means the ability to respond, or not, to a situation and is about looking at things from a higher point of view. By doing this we get a clearer image of what's going on. A co-creator with the God-force, you could say. That may sound simple, but it isn't as easy as it sounds, as we have been programmed for many lifetimes to think that we are puppets in this game of life.

We are not. We create our lives each day. We make decisions, we make choices all the time, and usually without realising it, and even not making a decision is in fact making one. The difference is, when you 'wake up' to this way of thinking, you become aware that you have a choice and that you're not a victim in life.

The more focus you give something, the more it grows, so living in the past is not a healthy way to live. But I hadn't realised that to live in a 'happy past' can be just as damaging as permanently thinking of an unhappy past. I hadn't made that connection until I read Carolyn Myss, and she gave me the missing piece of my jigsaw: to keep thinking of what it was like when you were happy, is just as damaging as thinking of unhappy times.

Once people are aware of the possibility of being able to create their journey, they are excited and usually make big changes in their life. This could be why many relationships break up. Once they know their happiness is at stake, they don't want to waste any more time. Books are sought after, classes and workshops are attended and, at first, it feels good as we soak up the new information, just like a sponge, wanting more and more of this new way of thinking. We can't wait to find what to do next and how to do it, as to see the change in ourselves is very empowering.

Sometimes, though, something really big happens in that change and it may get a little tough. Things start to get difficult and chaotic, and our faith in it all can be lost. This tends to be the turning point for many people. They decide they have had enough and this way of thinking isn't for them, but faith in a higher source is easy when life is good and when our vibrations are high.

It is when things go 'wrong' that we need faith, and yet that seems to be when we lose it. We could ask ourselves how much we really believe what we have read/heard, etc.? We all want what I now call 'The Diane Cooper experience' (where she was at her lowest point and was about to give up when she saw an angel in her room. She received a message that started her on the journey she is now on as 'The Angel lady').

> '*There are only two ways to live your life. One is as though nothing is a miracle. The other is as though everything is a miracle.*'
> Albert Einstein

Sadly, not many of us have an experience like that, although in my dark moments I have spit my dummy out at 'them upstairs' as to why when my life has been in turmoil I didn't get such a vision or voice advising me what to do. Sometimes, at my worst moments, especially in the year of finishing this book, it was like the universe had turned against me; it was almost saying 'let's hit her with all we have and see what she does about it'. Everything that could have gone wrong did. I now realise I shouldn't have been DOING anything!

We spend much of our energy doing things, instead of using that energy for our Self. When a crisis hits us, it has come to attract our attention to something that needs addressing in our life. As soon as we find the button that was pressed to bring up the emotions that need looking at, we find the situation calms back down and goes away; of course, how quickly depends on how quickly we find the solution.

In my last crisis I just couldn't get a grip and it took me into one of the deepest pits I have been in. I was there for a long time, and it literally brought me to my knees. I believed I was following my signs and getting along in life nicely, but things just started going against me.

My business started failing, and I knew I had some big decisions to make. However, I just couldn't get my head around why this was happening to me. I seemed to be losing people from my life, too, as many of my relationships were breaking up. The more I tried to work out what was happening, the worse it got.

I ended up doing exactly what I talked about in previous chapters and started to blame other people, then my guides, and finally, I blamed God and went into the whirlwind of depression; and that brought more dis-harmony to my life and obviously my body. The further into the pit I fell, the greater my problems became. Of course, my body started to reflect this (as it does – it only wants to make me happy) and I became a huge ball of FEAR (I even reflected the 'huge' part, as I gained much weight).

Needless to say, I didn't think of writing; after all, what was the point? How could I write about how to create what you want in life when my own life had fallen apart?

> '*Whenever a door closes, a new one always opens*.' Helen Keller,
> Deaf-blind US Author and Activist

This spell lasted for over two months, but seemed like two years.

The worse I got, the less I worked with the crystals or anything else, so obviously my energy reduced and the spiral continued. After what seemed like a lifetime, I surrendered and gave up the fight, as that is what it had become, a fight. I told God I'd had enough and was packing 'it' in. I was returning to 'normal'.

As soon as I did I started to feel better. My depression slowly lifted and I knew to get my crystals out to work with them. As my energy started to grow, my thoughts became clearer. I picked up my book and started to read my own words. I lived it daily until I was back on my feet and returning to full power.

My children later laughed at the thought of me not working with metaphysics.

'How can you give up something that IS you?' they asked.

After falling in the 'pit' I *felt* I was back where I'd started thirty years ago, at the beginning of the game of snakes and ladders we call life. Only this time I saw it from a different viewpoint – I had a clean slate. What did I want to do with it? What did I want to create?

Wondering what the previous couple of years had been about, I set about making a new life. This time, instead of wanting to go abroad or travel the world, I wanted nothing more than what I'd had four years ago – a home, my family and friends and a fulfilling career.

So I started again from scratch, but this time I was more aware to only create what I DID want in my life. As I started asking myself what I wanted, I began to get excited instead of scared, realising I could have any life I wanted. Yes, I could move abroad. I could get a job. I could change careers altogether. I could do anything I wanted.

This was an exciting position to be in, but also scary, as I knew where I'd gone wrong. I'd been sending out messages to the universe for so many different things I wanted; no wonder I had had such confusion in my life.

I'd been asking to live abroad, yet I wanted to travel the country doing seminars; I also wanted to stay home baking cakes for my grandchildren. I was creating such conflicting dreams, how could the universe bring me peace?

So the 'breakdown' of my life turned out to be a blessing (as they usually do).

I woke early one morning and everything seemed so clear. I realised that in the last year of drama, I'd changed the name of the book to 'Creating Reality', and in doing so I was doing what the title said: creating my reality.

> '*The mind is its own place, and in itself, can make heaven of Hell, and a hell of Heaven.*' John Milton, English Poet

I was constantly going over the pages and literally bringing up the issues I was writing about. I was living the book! I felt like the boy in Never Ending Story where he's in the attic and can't get his head around the fact that as he reads the words, he lives them. I now understand why the computer kept going haywire. It was as if it was trying to let me know I was regurgitating my words, and as I did, I was reliving them.

The constant talking about (therefore focusing on) my fears, hurts and pains was causing them all to rise to the surface again and I was recreating them in my life. The scariest part of all this was that I was proving to myself that what I was writing about was the truth. Talk about a writer studying his project!

Once I had this realisation, I could get on with my life. I got out the rubber band to put on my wrist for when I had a negative thought and I started each day by creating the day I wanted. I set my intention. I designed a programme for myself, which I later called 'The ME programme', and started reading my own words and taking my own advice. And hey presto! It worked.

Here are a few ways to get your energy back up:

✳ Take a shower and picture the water as white light coming into the crown and washing through your body, letting the negativity be washed down the plughole (if you are a bath person you can put sea salt in the water, as the salt transmutes, and try to immerse your full body). Sea salt can also be placed in rooms that have a low energy, but remember to sweep or hoover them up after 24 hours.

✳ A walk in nature is another good way to restore your energy, especially if you touch a plant or tree and discharge your energy. I was fearful of this at first, as I felt it wasn't fair on the plant, but I later realised that plants actually thrive on this, as they transmute the energy before giving it back out to us. Also, go near the sea, as this gives off negative ions, and the sand is mainly quartz for positive energy.

✳ Sit with a crystal, or even better, lay down with crystals on and around your body (see back of book).

✳ To energise food and water, you can place clear quartz in food cupboards and in a glass you use for drinking water; this helps to keep the body in a charged state, clearing the negativity.

✳ Sit/lie with relaxation music on and breathe slowly.

I began to look at my food/drink intake, as I knew that too much caffeine can affect the energy system because it can lodge in the Etheric layer and sometimes in the mental and emotional layers, which can have an effect on the nervous system too. Alcohol interferes with the astral body and can affect the personality, and when alcohol and caffeine are taken in great quantities, the heart chakra will be damaged.

I looked at the effect of chemicals in my environment too; I realised that I had storage heaters and when I researched some of the side effects, I must say I was alarmed at how money is put before human health.

Most importantly, I finally found peace again and made friends with myself, but most importantly, I gave myself a break from the constant picking at my faults. I allowed myself to be human! When that moment of peace returned I was so pleased. I had begun to wonder if I'd ever feel it again. Hitting rock bottom is a good point from which to make a new start; after all, the only way to go is up!

But why do we have to wait so long before we can have the courage to say we're not happy? Why do we often wait until a partner drives us to despair, or a really bad illness hits us? If we were honest with ourselves and loved ourselves enough, we'd know we were not happy. We owe it to ourselves to do something to change the situation, instead of waiting until it's beyond repair. Many of us even blame another person for the problem that we've known was there for a while.

Surely, if I believe that I am a co-creator with the God-force, I have no reason to wait for the universe to bring me the things I ask for and I can create them for myself. All I need is the belief! And if I don't get what I want, I can't have believed I deserved it in first place.

Can you imagine if we all balanced our lives and worked on world peace together? Just think of it! Unfortunately, so many of us are running around looking for answers to make our lives whole. We're like fishes swimming in the sea looking for water. My friend once heard an international speaker say:

'I've read hundreds of books and attended hundreds of workshops; why aren't I enlightened?' But exactly what does enlightened mean? It just means that we have the 'light' and light = information. Once we have the information, we are not so scared.

Being informed means having the choice. Having a choice gives us back the power and the responsibility of our actions, therefore our life. Being in the dark is what frightens us the most. When we are not told what is happening, we can start to make up stories in our heads, and yet usually, when we have all the facts, the reality isn't half as bad as we thought.

I'm really pleased I didn't go back to my old way of thinking, as the last fifteen years since having my first healing have probably been among the happiest in my life, yet at the same time confusing, painful and frustrating.

I found myself switching heads regularly, wondering which one I should wear that day, and on a bad day I'd think I'd lost the plot completely. But on a good day, I feel such bliss and I do truly love who I am, as those of you who have reached that point will be able to relate to. I've learnt who I am and that I do have choices in my life, and for me at this moment I'm doing what's right for me. I'm walking my (sometimes rocky) path, but it's the path that leads me to my true self. I also now realise that there's a difference between knowing your path and walking the path!

> '*What lies behind us, and what lies before us, are tiny matters compared to what lies within us.*' Oliver Wendell Holmes, American Poet, Writer and Physician

Our thoughts and beliefs are so powerful, and they can rule or ruin our life, as we live the life we want as we think it. That's how it's shown in the film What Dreams May Come with Robin Williams. So, if we are powerful enough to create what we want in a dream state, it has to be in the physical world that we 'block' things.

Let's face it, your body can go for a short nap and while you're there for maybe 15 minutes you can have a dream that spans a couple of days (in dream time). That shows us that we have no time in spirit! Could it mean that this is the dimension where we create what we want in life?

Somehow, in dream state we create what we want instantly, because we don't have a physical body to drag around to accomplish the task in hand. That's how it is when we die, too. So, if you are trying to create something in your life and are not managing to bring it into your life, look back to the chakra information and see the journey that the desire has to take to be accomplished – through GOD.

God

I have tried many times to get an idea of what God is. Once, while I was in India, I pictured a huge father figure (no gender intended) and his heart was filled with so much loving energy that he felt he would burst (anyone with a child will know how this feels), and burst is exactly what he/it did. That expansion of heart energy is what we are, loving energy of the God-force (that's how I term the Big Bang).

But because religion has led us to believe that God is a superpower and that we must look *up to it*, we think 'it' is outside of us. But love is not an external thing; it's in every living life force. *Every child born is pure love.*

It is human conditioning that changes that statement. Let us change it for the better! All you have to do is think differently about yourself and by changing your view of yourself, you will learn to understand what makes you tick, and when you get to know the true YOU, you'll love yourself, warts and all.

'GOD' is body, mind and spirit in harmony, and as thoughts become reality when they are thought enough times, when we get 'our act together' (mind, body and soul) we have the energy from the three parts of our self.

God starts in the head area with a thought (GENERATED) and then comes down into the throat area to be expressed. This centre is where we 'walk our talk'. So we talk about what we want to create, and we give it life (energy) to bring it into the physical reality. The vibrations leaving the third eye and throat will also include the ear chakras, as communication is a two-way thing.

So, the journey of the creation now has to travel down to the heart area.

If the person who first created the thought doesn't bring in this project soon, others can pick it up and create it (this could explain the ideas that I and my children have had over the years, but someone else had invented them), as it's in the ether, so the energy is now floating somewhere.

We hold our hopes, dreams, fears and emotions about guilt, grief, resentment, etc. in the heart, so what happens to our dream/desire at this stage will depend on any blockages we have in this area (ORGANISE).

Our dream can often get lost at this stage, as our energy has moved the desire down and has to start clearing out any left baggage to make way for the new (just as if it were a house you had moved into, you would clear away anything that had been left behind). Depending on how much baggage has been sitting there will depend on how long you have spent clearing it.

Once that's done, the energy/desire will move down to the solar plexus area and again will need a clear-out to make way for the desire. This area is where we find out if we feel worthy of it, as we decide if we have the confidence to carry it out.

Remember also, that the further towards the earth chakra we get the heavier the energy becomes, so the energy will carry more weight now, making it harder to shift.

The solar plexus is also where our inner child resides, so any held emotions of not being loved or not being good enough will be stored here. At this stage, feelings may come up and ask 'who do you think you are?' or tell you 'you can't do that'. These and many more doubts come to remind you of the programming you may have had as a child.

Depending on how much needs clearing will decide whether we can even be bothered to go ahead with it at all, and this is usually where a lot of desires get binned as being a daft idea anyway.

> *'If I believe I cannot do something, it makes me incapable of doing it. But when I believe I can, then I acquire the ability to do it, even if I did not have the ability in the beginning.'* Mahatma Gandhi

I believe this is where a lot of dreams 'die', so if you are not giving the idea energy the creation will fade and cease to exist for you. However, someone else could pick it up from the floating sea of energy in the astral.

If at this point you have not given up, the desire will be brought down to the sacral area. This is where we create things, including life, and the desire hasn't far to go now.

So now we work through any issues to do with expressing ourselves (including sexuality) and once again, this area usually needs a good clear out, as we've become a generation of people with many guilt issues. But once these are dealt with, the energy only has to go down to the base chakra and it has arrived.

It actually becomes a reality! (DELIVERED) We have achieved what we first dreamt of. We end up with the desired result. Thanks to the system we call GOD.

GENERATED
ORGANISED
DELIVERED

Of course, the desire could look rather different from the original, depending on the journey it's taken through your system and how long it took to get to this stage, but in some shape or form, it's created.

I find that when I'm abroad and in the sun/sand setting I am probably at my peak. My energy is especially well balanced while travelling, as I have no responsibility, so my energy is pretty much mine. Therefore, to have a desire at that point is easy, as I don't have much blocking my system.

In that state I believe I can achieve anything, and because I have so much enthusiasm (God within), I have the power to create the dream. It's only when I'm back in my hometown that hiccups occur with my creations.

By then, I'm in the energy of my emotions and doubts that are held in my fears and back with the people and areas that constantly remind me of memories of past fears and doubts.

I also pick up and carry others' fears and doubts as I walk around, as I take on the consciousness of the town. Whether my dream becomes a reality depends on how quickly I act when I return. Obviously, I acted quickly with my new shop, as it became physical.

On my return, everything fell into place, with appointments being available, the exact money being there, even dates on all the paperwork falling into place. However, about a month after opening I started to dip in energy (obviously because I'd worked such long hours decorating a three-storey building) and I started having doubts about what I'd done and why.

These thoughts haunted me literally and would have to take the same route as my dreams had. So my thoughts and emotions were affected. Then my physical body became rather ill at one point. My energy would now have to be used to keep myself afloat, rather than going further into the pit of despair.

At first, I couldn't see what was happening, I just thought I was doing my best to survive the situation and, as I got my power back more and more, my energy started returning to its full potential. Then I was able to look back and see what had caused that particular dip.

Although much of what had been coming at me was from an outside source (a certain radical group were threatening my business), I must take full responsibility for my own energy being so low in the first place to allow it in. If my energy had been high, the darkness that engulfed me would not have been able to penetrate my aura.

My energy had become low due to the physical work, but it was also due to an emotional issue going on with me since I'd returned to my hometown. I had a particular painful situation going on that really brought me to my knees. There was also emotional drainage taking place due to my youngest son, my baby, leaving town to go and live in London. Fear came in and resided in my heart, bringing up a very old fear of losing my children. This old fear (apparently a common one) had been around for many years and, as with all fears, it decided to pop up to say hi!

Our fears reside in our system while they still have an effect on us, but once we are not affected by them, they dissolve. Mine obviously hadn't, as my son going to London became a really painful time for me.

As I was crying constantly, most people thought I was over-reacting because of the terrorist bombings that had been torturing our capital. But it was simply that I was going to miss my child so much and not get to see him pop through the door and say hi, with his gorgeous smile and hug that made my day.

What I didn't realise was that the actual core of my fear of not seeing him went much deeper, as I found out in therapy. I'd almost lost him in childbirth and was told many times by the nurses that if I had been five minutes later getting to the hospital he would have died. I'd kept putting off going to the hospital (as I had already been admitted four times during the pregnancy) and didn't want to be a bother to my husband again, as he had been called away from work on a few occasions.

I'd carried the pain of nearly losing my child with me all those years.

Looking into this issue, I also realised that the fear went even further back, I believed I didn't deserve the 'happy ever after' life.

> *'Whether you believe you can do a thing or not, you are right.'*
> Henry Ford, Ford Motor Company

I sometimes refer to what's happening on earth to the film Star Wars, the dark fighting the light. Looking at the world today, this doesn't seem so difficult to believe; if the darkness rules, it is mission accomplished for the dark side.

The fact that we are often controlled by fear, etc. means that we in turn give out that frequency, which in turn feeds the energy that controls us. In this state we do not feel love, as it's impossible to feel love when we are in fear mode, as love is a different vibration to fear. Love = high. Fear = low.

In order to change our lives we need to give the subject of 'me' a lot more attention. Instead of looking around at others and pointing out what is wrong in another person's life, we must look to the self first. Perhaps that is where the story of Jesus and 'casting the first stone' came from.

We simply haven't been educated with this information, and therefore grow up thinking that life just happens to us, as if that man is sat 'up there' choosing who to be kind to and who to be horrible to.

I do think the majority of us know this isn't true, and if the real ancient teachings from the great masters such as Jesus, Mohammed and Buddha were followed, we would realise this and create the life and world we would prefer to live in. After all, we were told things like: 'These and more you can do for yourself'.

We need to raise our vibrations and face our fears, remembering who we really are and what our dreams are. Therefore, it has to start with the self. How else can we move on if we don't do this? Once we accept ourselves, we start to make friends with ourselves; we start to love ourselves.

As this happens, the peace we feel will bring about changes in our thoughts, emotions and also our physical body. The changes will start to occur in the body and we will take on higher and higher frequencies as our bodies go through this transformation, trying to accommodate these energies, so we must learn how to handle it.

> '*You will not be punished for your anger; you will be punished by your anger.*' The Buddha, Founder of Buddhism

A common emotion when these changes occur is one of something being missing from life or a sadness that just won't go away, which in turn leads to a feeling of fear. All of our bodies (aura) feel the changes, particularly our emotional body, which seems to go to pot, for which we usually blame our hormones, etc.

The mental body often thinks we're having a breakdown, and in some senses we are – a breakdown in the old systems. The physical body is affected, as the nervous system has to hold so much frequency.

It's understandable why some people decide to opt out and stay as they are; it often seems easier that way and that's okay for those who do; after all; it's our life to do with as we wish. And it's your life to do with as YOU wish.

All you need to do is trust what you feel is right for you...

Not me, your therapist or doctor, the priest or the latest book, but YOU.

CHAPTER 10

Body Language

WHEN SOME PEOPLE become ill they seem to think it's been dropped on them from above. Of course, it doesn't happen that way, but we have become a culture of blamers and we tend to shift our attention to another person, or body. It becomes the fault of our partners, friends, employers, the system or, if all else fails, GOD (even for those who don't believe in him/it). But then pain does that, doesn't it?

It makes us weak and when we are weak we have no energy, and this can make us 'powerless'. Many people have become lazy by giving power to anyone who'll sort it, be it our partners, doctors or the government, in fact, anyone who'll give us the solution, instead of finding the answers for ourselves.

The fact is, the human body is self-repairing and self-healing when not in a state of stress. Stress is a word we are all too familiar with and most people will have suffered from it at some point in their life. Stress is the manifestation of how we handle a situation and some people deal with it better than others. But stress is simply a word we use when we lose our confidence in being able to deal with the task facing us.

> '*When you make the two one, and when you make the inside like the outside and the outside like the inside, and the above like the below, and when you make the male and the female one and the same ... then you will enter the Kingdom of God.*' Jesus of Nazareth.

The lives many people are leading at the moment involve so much stress! And stress is a killer if not taken seriously, as our adrenal glands produce certain hormones. In fact, these glands help our body deal with stress, and whenever your body is under stress these glands produce cortisol (the stress hormone), as I found out only too well when I was going through my self-destruct period.

Cortisol is a very important hormone, as when in the right balance it's vital to your survival. Studies have shown that every cell in your body has receptors for cortisol, which means that cortisol 'talks' to every cell in your body, switching its metabolic processes on and off when needed.

Problems occur when we have too much or too little cortisol too often. Once again, this will cause an imbalance in our system. Our body knows when something isn't right for us, but we simply do not stay still long enough to be able to hear its messages. I know I wish I'd listened to mine more often when I was going through my loss, because as I didn't, for the first time in my life I started suffering with my stomach.

Eventually, the doctors found I had something called Helicobacter Pylori, which I'd never heard of. Yet, when I told others, they seemed to have had it or known someone who had. The medication I was given actually made me worse, as it stripped my immune system and caused many side effects. The whole scenario was horrendous to go through, so I started researching 'The little squatter', as I termed it.

The facts I came across were very scary, including learning how many people have it without even knowing. As if that fact wasn't bad enough, it is able to survive the gastric acids in the stomach due to its ability to produce an enzyme called urease, which can neutralise stomach acid, allowing it to survive in its own acid-free zone. It actually penetrates the stomach's protective mucous lining by burrowing in, as it is shaped like a corkscrew.

These are scary facts and I'm not scare mongering, but the link between this bacteria and stressful lifestyles must be made public before the situation gets any worse. Personally, I don't think enough is being done to try and sort this, as I know that the percentage success rate for the mainstream antibiotics isn't high enough.

I have spent a fortune on natural remedies, which have helped enormously, but I must say it didn't happen with the backing of some of my doctors. In fact, one actually laughed in my face when I told him I wanted to cure it using natural products. Yet, since 2000, the number of prescriptions issued have increased by 22% to over 600 million, costing the NHS 50% more than ten years ago.

The more cortisol we have the more stressed we feel, as this reduces our immune system, which makes us more susceptible to illness and dis-ease. When we are stressed our body pumps toxins into the bloodstream, which deplete the body of vitamins, minerals and other nutrients. Therefore, we must start taking more responsibility for our health by reducing stress from our lives and by looking into new ways to be healthy.

'Health is our greatest wealth.' Ralph Waldo Emerson, American Poet

The Health and Safety Executive estimated that self-reported work-related stress, depression or anxiety accounts for approximately 10.5 million reported lost working days per year in Britain. The Psychosocial Working Conditions (PWC) surveys indicated that around 1 in 6 of all working individuals thought their job was very or extremely stressful. These are statistics we shouldn't ignore.

We have an innate wisdom, the subconscious mind, whose job it is to tie in and synchronise all the activities in the body, but when that communication system is broken down and not functioning properly, it will not matter how healthy each organ is, you won't have good health, as if you affect one aspect of yourself, you affect all the other aspects to different degrees.

Re-establishing the mind/body balance reduces allergies, emotional and psychological disorders and many other illnesses. It also improves posture, coordination, digestion, brain functions and learning disorders. Most importantly, it balances the states of distorted viewpoints (negative belief systems and attitudes), bringing harmony to the system.

More people are now deciding to stand up for injustices in the health field, while others are deciding to start a new life when the old one isn't making them happy. Many are downsizing and getting back to basics, while others are looking at the importance of health, the foods we eat and the exercise we take. These are all good moves, but we could look closer at the metaphysical view of some problems we come across.

Take a situation with the stomach when you've eaten something that doesn't agree with you. That in itself should be telling you something, because if your stomach chakra was strong it would sort itself out without becoming a physical problem. If the chakra is weak, your body will 'talk' to you by giving you a tummy upset to tell you it needs balancing.

You might find no reason for a headache, but on taking a closer look you may find you've simply been stretching your mind too much, or thinking about things you really don't want to think about.

If you are short of breath, ask yourself if you've been stressed (remember, stress is just a word we use when we lose our confidence in our ability to deal with the situation we're in), as stress will bring on shallow breathing. Once you stop, relax and breathe deeply for a while and it should self-repair. However, if the problem doesn't clear and the body doesn't return to normal, we must ask why and take it further by looking back over previous days to see what you'd been feeling. If emotions of anger, fear, guilt and resentment (low frequencies) were in your system, within a few days it will have had an effect on you physically.

If you ignore your intuition, you will create tension in your system, which will eventually lead to unhappiness. This is your body's way of attracting attention to the area that needs looking at. When you have 'rooted' the issue, the energy is released, allowing the area to return to free-flowing energy and bringing harmony to the situation/body.

When there is tension in our thoughts or beliefs, we will experience it in the chakra, which will affect the endocrine gland, which then secretes hormones, changing the chemistry in the body part.

As we direct energy with thought (where thought goes, energy flows), we have the power to unblock whatever thought created the tension in the first place. When energy flows freely we have wholeness; when energy is blocked we have tension. When we don't accept a part of who we are, what we did or what we are doing, there can be a reversal in our energy system. The outcome is an unconscious act to sabotage our dreams and desires.

> 'Our central nervous system contains from 10 to 100 million cells, each one of which has a storage capacity equal to that of a large computer.' Alexander Rich, American Biologist and Biophysicist

When thought forms go into the ether (which is between the physical and spiritual realms), they go into something similar to a hologram and the thoughts stay there until the conditions are right to manifest on earth. So it's very important to watch our thoughts and also the language we use, as they both carry very powerful vibrations.

When I traced the root of my destruction period, I traced it to a comment that a customer had made to me at a show at which I was presenting. It immediately 'hooked' into a deep fear I'd carried for most of my life; that I'd done something wrong! The customer had implied that I'd done an injustice to someone when I opened my second shop. I didn't want to cause a scene, so I didn't tell her the truth that in fact I'd had the injustice.

When I got home this played over and over in my mind. It simply wouldn't go away, and as the universe is magnetic, I began attracting similar vibrations into my life. The next day I had a rare visit from a cousin who asked how the show went. This brought me to the comment and pulled me deeper into a discussion on the subject; we actually fell out that day, as he confessed that he thought the same. I was defending my actions continually, but at least ended by telling him the truth about the situation.

However, although I told my cousin the truth, I couldn't believe that he had thought I would do such a thing. The self-destruct phase that followed was huge. On some level I must have believed what they'd said to me, as eventually, I destroyed everything I'd created. Not only did I destroy my success, I destroyed myself in the process. I felt like I 'd lost my spirit, which affected my mind and body.

The full destruction cycle took three years exactly to the month and the three years that follow will finish just in time for the equinox of 2012; and God only knows what will be happening in the world by then.

People think that because of my experience with angels and guides I shouldn't be having all this chaos, and at the beginning that's how I felt too. But this is my journey, and for whatever reason, I have my experiences to learn, in whatever way I choose to learn them.

I actually know that I'm a spirit energy that's focused in this physical body simply for the ride, but recently, I have declared to my soul that I'd like to start learning a little more through joy rather than pain. Of course, it will depend on how much I believe I deserve it!

Look again at the liver; when we can't face life, we often turn to drink, etc. which when really abused can turn to liver failure, so by not getting our feelings sorted we store the frustration/anger in our liver chakra. But remember, our feelings and symptoms have come to tell you something!

> 'The only thing that can grow is the thing you give energy to.'
> Ralph Waldo Emerson

Is there a part of you that isn't too pleased with yourself? Have you been acting out of character? Have you been unkind or cruel to someone, or more commonly have you been scared of something? Do you want to be or do something else and feel you can't because you have responsibilities (this would make you feel trapped, which will trap your energy)?

When we become nervous or scared our body reacts, as we have the flight or fight mode and therefore breathe differently and tend to move our awareness (shift our energy) into the past or the future. Just when we need all the help we can get we put our energy elsewhere, which leaves us even more disempowered, as remember, where thought goes, energy flows.

When our thoughts go to the past or the future, that's where our energy is directed and therefore, we cannot be at our best. It's like trying to run a radio using half-charged batteries – we wouldn't be able to get the best sound from the machine, only a slow distorted one. The body is just the same, and if not fully charged we give off a slow vibration and will not be working on full power.

So a problem with the stomach could show us that we have an issue with self-esteem/confidence or personal power. The liver stores energy (which also includes anger and this is often linked to cancer). Our waterworks are part of the kidney system and skin, and are governed by the same chakra, representing emotions.

> '*We have to use language to communicate our inner experience which in its very nature transcends linguistics.*' D. T. Suzuki, Buddhist Author and Essayist

So look back at the few days before the problem started and see what you were doing or feeling at the time. Were you feeling powerless? Did you go against your gut feeling in a situation? Were you frightened of something/ someone, or even of yourself? Did you not take control in a situation, or did you want to but your inner child was scared so you let the moment pass? These and many more reasons could be the underlying cause of your stomach ache.

The mouth is another weak spot where things are going wrong within the system. Many people are still having problems with honesty (especially with themselves) and physically, the mouth is where digestion begins. Not many of us chew our food enough and chewing starts the saliva, which is vital so that the enzymes can be released to break down fats and starches. It also tells the stomach that proteins are on the way.

Metaphysically, we don't chew over our words before speaking them or before taking in what others have said, and if we 'chewed' it over, we would get used to what is about to come into our system.

Physically, our stomach is where we churn over our food (energy supply) and metaphysically where we digest what is happening to us.

The pancreas produces the hormone insulin that flows into the bloodstream to go round the body to help entry of glucose cells. *Metaphysically, this is where we look at how much sweetness and joy we have in our lives.*

The liver secretes 700ml of bile daily, which is stored in the gallbladder. The bile breaks down the fat so that it can be chemically separated by the juices of the pancreas before entering the bloodstream.

Metaphysically, our liver is where we store our energy. If this is not released in a productive manner it will remain stored here; as mentioned earlier, anger is often stored here too, and if not dealt with this can lead to many problems later in life, including cancer.

So what can be done if we have a problem? You could pop to a chemist for something to mask the pain/symptom, but remember that your body always wants to please you; therefore, if you respect it and look after it, and feed it well by putting good fuel into it, it will always respond in a loving way.

If you liken your body to a supermarket trolley, how do you shop? Do you rush round and throw anything in, or do you take your time and put in only the best? It's vital that we begin to realise how important an effect our diet has on our body. Our health problems may be caused by the food we do or do not eat, even though we now have many good TV programmes to educate us on this subject.

A long time ago we would have grown our own food and known the journey the food had taken to get to the table. Today, we buy from supermarkets and don't know its journey. My own relationship with food has changed greatly since I studied subtle energies and the interaction of our bodies with the environment.

I try not to eat food from the microwave (for obvious reasons), or processed and GM foods if I can help it. I also had to look at gluten, as bloating became a problem, and when I looked into it, once again it made sense, as it sticks to the bowel (like glue). My food consists mainly of fresh vegetables, but I do eat meat on occasions, although not very often, as it sits in the gut for weeks. I once heard someone say that 'she didn't want to be a cow's graveyard'; after that I turned vegetarian for a couple of years, as her words stuck with me for a long time.

I usually eat fresh, simple foods, saving more complex food for dining out. This way I find a good balance that keeps me happy and usually healthy.

However, if I'm ill in any way, I always look to the body chart and see what it's trying to tell me, and with the exception of the previously mentioned problems, I can usually sort it out.

I've found that many people will come into the holistic way of thinking only after trying all the conventional ways. I am the other way round. I will try chemical medication only if I cannot or choose not to get to the root of the issue.

A lot of people are now questioning tablets in general and often look for the alternative. The fact that people are looking at prevention instead of cure is, I believe, a good way forward for us all.

'We are at once the creators of our reality and the victims of our creation.' Fred Alan Wolf, Quantum Theorist

A man I have much respect for is Martin Brofman. In one of his articles he wrote about his doctor telling him that he had just one or two months to live, unless he coughed or sneezed, in which case he could die immediately.

Instead of reading how he was preparing for his death, I read that he'd learnt about the subtle bodies and how to self-heal. He studied the ancient systems of healing and has now taught how to self-heal for the last 22 years.

He quotes in his book:

'So now I do what makes me happy and if I feel unhappy doing something, I stop doing it. I have a little internal alarm clock I use. My feeling is that I should always be able to say I love where I am, I love whom I'm with and I love what I'm doing. If at any time I don't feel comfortable saying this, I know I have to change something. If I don't love where I am, I know I need to be somewhere else, and I leave. If I don't love being with the person in that moment then I know our vibrations are not compatible for that moment and I know I must either be alone or with someone else – and I act on that. If I don't feel comfortable saying I love what I am doing I know I must do something else, and I do. I spend time with those I feel good with not living by social obligation. My friends are those with whom I feel a personal connection, not those I feel I "should" be with to further my career.'

His book *Anything Can Be Healed* is a great read, and if we all lived by this rule I think the world would be a happier place, as we'd be free to be who we really are. But how many people are living a life because they think they should, and not because they are truly happy in it?

Taoist sages say that when you smile your organs release a honey-like secretion that nourishes the whole body, and when you are angry, fearful or under great stress, they produce a poisonous secretion which blocks up the energy channels. They practice what is known as the 'inner smile'.

When our body is stressed, we prepare for fight or flight continuously, and our body comes under great pressure. We are always preparing for an emergency that never happens. To worry creates the situation in the mind, and therefore the body goes through the same stages, leaving it in a state of a quickening heartbeat, dilated pupils, tightened muscles, adrenalin released into the bloodstream, a rise in blood pressure and a suppressed immune system.

When we think a thought, three billion cells follow suit! If we imagine it to be, then it is so, and our body will act automatically. Yes, if we imagine something in our mind, then we have sent a message telling our body we have a problem and the body will act accordingly. Therefore, our body mirrors who we are to the outside world.

If you're a worrier, go for walk, jog or whatever it takes to release the pent-up energy. If you're not good at the exercise thing, find a couple of songs that have a really good effect on you. They may remind you of better times, or when they were around perhaps you were in a good place in your life. Put them on and just dance around the room, or just twist, as this relieves stress. And it makes you feel good just to release the energy that's making you feel sluggish or down in the dumps.

Another good way is to begin and end each day with a breathing programme: make yourself comfortable, sit and relax yourself, and breathe slowly seven times. With each breath, imagine a colour going into the chakra. Start with the base and breathe in the colour red; picture a ball of bright, vibrant red swirling around this area. Work your way up the chakras, with the colour being breathed in and around the area, and end with the crown and imagine the colour purple.

This will bring balance and harmony into your system and can be done at any time of day and as often as you like. It's especially good to use when something stresses you out. Just remember to breathe slowly and calm will come to you. If you ever do this regime and it doesn't bring the calm you desire, look deeper at the issue. Is there a deeper reason for the stress? Remember, your ego may try to tell you there's no point in doing it.

> '*The light can be switched on in an instant. The true question, and also the challenge, is how long it will take you to find the switch.*' James Arthur Ray.

There are many self-help tools around, including classes and workshops, but it was very different years ago when I was in need of help. The only book I could find in the library was *Out on a Limb* by Shirley McLean. I didn't know it was going to be a helpful book; I only borrowed it because I liked her as an actress. Yet, it became a much-loved book of mine and later a video, which I lent to many people, but I am sure each of you will find your own love.

Some people tune into crystals, some to soft music or angels and many other subjects that appeal. You may find that you are attracted to the Native American culture or Buddha's, etc. Whichever you are drawn to, just make sure you approach it with fun and not with the attitude of work.

The journey of self-discovery should be a joyous one, at the end of which you will find out who you really are, and once you find that person you'll understand what a truly beautiful soul you are. Remember, this is a discovery of the SELF, which means you, not another person – just YOU.

Many people are looking for their Twin Soul or Soul Mate, thinking it will make life better, but I believe that the twin soul is in fact inside, the two parts of the self marrying together to make the complete self, as the heart chakra marries the two parts of the self together = top (spiritual) and lower (earth).

It makes more sense for *me* not to have to run around looking for that special someone who will make life complete, and for those who never find this person think life's passing them by. Once we have married our parts together and become one with our self, we can be more intuitive and sensitive, and life will become brighter.

We will also use our rational side more, making better choices in life, as when we believe in our self rather than in others, things start to flow with ease, we have harmony in our life and we can go with the flow of the universe.

My journey has turned out to be a precious gift for me. The young *Border girl really believed she wasn't worthy of real love and never thought she was good enough, a girl who has survived so much emotional, mental, physical and sexual abuse in childhood, as well as in adulthood, but who now *finally* realises she's as beautiful on the outside as on the inside and that she has so much to give to the world.

Since coming back home, starting another business, then losing it again through yet another 'accident' and having to heal and start all over again, I've been called an inspiration by many and I'm constantly told how happy people are to have me back in their lives. What a compliment! After all, I'm just ME. But maybe that's all I need to be! Me just being me! After all, I wouldn't be the 'me' I am without all the pain and suffering I've had. I wouldn't be the vibration I am. I'd be a different energy system altogether.

Mind you, at those times when my energy is low and my 'little devil' tells me it's all useless, I'll give myself a hard time by asking myself how I can believe that what I'm doing can be of any use. Or when all else fails and I don't give in to the taunting of 'no one loves you or 'your life is not going anywhere', or whatever else my 'devil' throws at me.

When I first started looking at this way of thinking, I wondered whether the authors of the books I was reading had ever had problems, as they seemed to have very peaceful, successful lives. I certainly can't say that, as my life's still unfolding and as I sit here writing I'm still sorting out my issues.

This seems to be an ongoing thing for me (but then I did have a *programme* of thinking that if something is worthwhile, we have to work hard for it). I can honestly say that most of the time I see my life issues in a completely different way than I used to, therefore making them easier to work through, and I have also noticed that they don't come around too often either.

I was given the verse on the following page from my hypnotherapy teacher, Norma, and I thought I'd share it with you. It would do us all good to read it regularly.

The term Border Girl is used because I came from an area of poverty over the railway lines.

I LOVE MYSELF

I love myself the way I am
There's nothing I need to change
There is nothing to rearrange
I'm beautiful and capable
Of being the best me I can and
I love myself just the way I am
I love you the way you are
There's nothing you need to do
When I feel the love inside myself
It's easy to love you
Behind your fears, your rage and tears
I see your shining star and
I love you just the way you are
I love the world the way it is
'Cause I can clearly see
That all the things I judge are done
By people just like me
So till the birth of peace on earth
That only love can bring

I'll help it grow by loving everything
I love myself the way I am
And still I want to grow
But change outside can only come
When deep inside I know
I'm beautiful and capable
Of being the best me I can
And I love myself just the way I am
I love myself just the way I am

Jai Josefs

A fitting verse, I thought! But unfortunately, we won't always be in a place where we can read it and believe it. However, if we keep working on loving ourselves, we will. Perhaps the most important question for us to heal our life is: Am I TRULY happy? If you can say yes from the heart, then everything should be ok with your life. If you can't, just ask why. What is missing or wrong with life? Ask simple questions such as:

'When did this feeling start?'

Look at your body and your life and see what it's trying to point out to you.

If you're convincing yourself the illness/unhappiness has nothing to do with you, then I have to say you could be in denial, as if it's in your life it has somehow been drawn in by you, consciously or unconsciously.

> '*If you have love in your life, it can make up for a great amount of things that you lack. If you don't have it, nothing else will matter.*'
>
> Leo Buscaglia, Professor, Author and Lecturer

For instance, if you have a cold and can't see what you could gain from this situation (such as getting time off work), then look closer at what's going on in your life. It could be that you have so much going on in your head that it's become clogged up with the constant crap that goes through a mind each day.

When I say a problem may be linked to a childhood issue, I'm often told: 'But I've had a happy childhood; I wasn't hurt or abused'. However, it doesn't always have to be a major thing that happened in your past, and could be something simple such as overhearing a parent say to someone that they think you're getting chubby, which could easily stay in your subconscious mind until you're grown up. Then it could become a self-esteem or weight issue that seems to dog your life.

So please don't always think someone has to have had a horrific time to have problems with their past; sometimes, the illnesses most difficult to overcome are born of the simplest situations. Something to also remember is: what we fear the most comes to us, as we feed it energy!

'*As a man thinketh – so he is.*' Old Testament

When I began realising how powerful a thought is, I looked back over situations in my life. I began to remember that having a fire in my home had always been such a big fear of mine. After I'd divorced, I'd lie in bed and plan how I'd get my children out if we had a fire, as I was now solely responsible for their safety, and I'd replay this over and over in my mind.

Then one night I had a major realisation. I regressed back to a memory of my mother when she'd fallen asleep with a cigarette and the bed set alight

123

with us in it. Thankfully, she woke up in time and the fire was put out before it became too severe, but as a child, this was indeed a terrifying experience and one that obviously stayed with me subconsciously (on a lighter note, the good that came out of it was that I've never smoked).

Remember, all of this information is ongoing; we don't just learn it and then get on with life, this IS life. If I ever have a problem in my life, my friends and family say: 'Well, you have all the answers, do something about it,' and that's true, I do understand how 'I' work, but that doesn't stop me from having issues and problems, colds and aches just like everyone else. And writing this book certainly brought up many issues that I thought I'd made peace with!

I say making peace with because I think the term healing is misunderstood. It suggests that the problem will leave your system, but as I believe things in life make us who we are, how can they leave us? I think the way we see or feel about something is what gets healed, and we just change our view of it.

I know I must always walk my talk and I've learnt to understand myself more. I have learnt to be honest with others and myself, but most importantly, I've learnt to truly love myself for who I am, warts and all. The majority of the time, I'm completely happy with the energy I transmit.

'The greatest mistake a man can make is to be afraid of making one.' Elbert Hubbard, American Philosopher and Writer

However, when I have a crisis within I don't see it that way until I lift myself from the pit I've fallen into, and at such times I literally fall out with 'those upstairs', the system I call GOD. I fall out with God in just the same way that I'd fall out with a friend or family member, because for me that's how it is.

I tell him/it how unhappy I am and why I think I'm not being supported, and how I don't want to talk to him/it. And then, of course, when my tantrum is over, I apologise for my behaviour and, as with all people who love us, we make up and move on from the episode.

But when a situation won't go away, I have found that it usually involves forgiveness of some sort, and usually me needing to forgive myself. The subject of forgiveness is a touchy one, but vital to our recovery. When we begin to heal our lives and past hurts, we are often advised to go down the road of forgiving people for past events that have hurt us and caused us distress. I am aware that the subject is even more painful when it involves a child, but if our soul is here to experience emotions, good and bad, then surely there is no need for forgiveness. After all, from a soul point of view, it is about having a learning experience that the soul has asked for.

Remember, I'm speaking here about the soul aspect, not the human aspect, which will bring about a human emotion. For me, I've healed more of my own pain with the understanding that I've had of my other lives. When I had my first PLR (Past Life Regression) and visited my last life, I found I was a horrible, hard man who inflicted pain on my wife and family.

This was very hard for me to take in at the time, but I couldn't dismiss the feelings that came from the experience. Therefore, if that's the reason I chose this life, with the people coming in to help me understand how others felt because of my actions in the past, then the situation has worked perfectly.

Even more interesting is the fact that since I had my regression, I haven't found myself in so many situations where people are hurting me in the same way. I now know this is because of the like-attracts-like law of the universe. I do not need to bring those kinds of experiences into my life, as I have recognised them in myself.

The view of why we have painful lives is changing more and more, as people are looking at past life regression and coming to an understanding that we could have been the one who caused someone pain and suffering, and that maybe we need to know how the other person feels in a situation. It's like a play, and we are in it for the experience.

What an experience!

There is more on the subject of past lives later in the book.

NB: Please do not be offended if you are or know someone who cannot find the solution or is disabled, etc., as I'm not saying that someone born with a life-changing condition can suddenly change because of such suggestions. That is a much deeper issue and is addressed in many books on reincarnation, etc. that can often bring a sense of peace to someone who is suffering.

If you feel the need to visit the doctor, please do so; this book is not a suggestion to override the medical profession. I believe this information should go hand in hand with medical beliefs.

Chapter 11

Crystals

I KNEW NOTHING about crystals or their properties when I first came across their healing power. I'd been persuaded to go to Scotland with a friend after she had told me of a healing retreat near the Highlands. I'd heard how beautiful Scotland was, but I was not 'into such things' as healing and the like.

However, a few years earlier I'd been involved in a car crash and I was in so much pain that it didn't seem possible that my life could get any worse. As the pain grew, so did my resentment towards the taxi driver and the off-duty drunken policeman who had crashed into us, and with the resentment had grown my depression, anger, etc. The condition of my spine was controlling my life and making it a misery and also that of my children, so I went along for the ride more than anything.

While I was at the retreat, a lady came down to breakfast and brought with her a beautiful piece of amethyst. Although I admired it, I secretly thought she was a little potty when she told us all how much it had cost her husband! I couldn't understand how someone could pay so much money for a piece of 'stone'.

> '*Not that which goes into the mouth ruins a man; but that which comes out of his mouth.*' Jesus of Nazareth

I took my attention back to the book I was reading, but in the background I could hear her mentioning 'healing with crystals' and I turned my attention to the discussion she'd started. After listening to some of her experiences with crystals, I asked how I could buy one to help with the pain in my back.

What I didn't know was that a lady called Linda was part of this group; she was a teacher just passing through the village and said that shops were far and few between, but my friend and I still went looking. To my dismay,

Linda had been correct – there were no crystals in this very remote part of Scotland.

A couple of days later, I came down to breakfast and found a small paper bag on my table. When I asked what it was, I was told that Linda had left it for me when she'd passed back through the village. I couldn't understand why she'd left it for me, as I didn't know her; I'd never even spoken to her.

The lady who was in charge of breakfast told me that Linda had asked me to:

'Enjoy the quartz and let it change your life.'

I looked at this piece of clear 'stone' and thought the lady called Linda a little strange to be giving gifts to complete strangers. I blushed as I received the bag enclosing the gift, as I was not used to receiving gifts without having to give something in return (childhood programming again).

As the lady in charge cleared away the breakfast pots, I asked her to pass my thanks on to Linda when she saw her again. I later started asking questions of the lady with the amethyst and she offered to loan me a book on crystals so that I could learn more about their healing qualities. True to her word, when she returned home to Brighton she sent me the book, and I began on what turned out to be a fascinating journey into the world of semi-precious stones and the incredible things that can be achieved by bringing them into your life.

That was over fifteen years ago, and I can honestly say that if I ever ran into Linda again (not that I would have a clue as to who she was) I would thank her with all my heart, as it literally did change my life.

It helped relieve the pain I was constantly in and I later found that, according to my children, I didn't 'lose it' so often, as my mood swings had become steadily worse over the years as the pain worsened and immobility became less. I became more powerless in what I could achieve and to have relief from this nightmare was literally a God-send.

But then I needed answers, as I started to be aware that my back was indeed a lot better. I couldn't understand it, as I'd seen the X-rays and I knew my spine was damaged with a crack at the base, a chip in the middle and the top four or five vertebrae crumbled. This was only a piece of crystal, how could this be happening?

> '*God sleeps in the rock, dreams in the plant, stirs in the animal ... and awakens in man.*' Ibn al Arabi, Muslim Mystic and Philosopher, Essayist and Lecturer

It had to all be in my head, as was said to me so often by people close to me.

They, too, couldn't understand the change in me, and it made no sense that a crystal could bring it about. To prove to myself that I was making it up (although I didn't care if it was in my head, I was just glad the pain had gone), I started looking for more books on the subject, but instead of *disproving* it, I saw more *proof*. For instance, I read that in Sweden they crush quartz and put it on the road at blackspots where a lot of accidents occur to raise the vibration.

Like me, you will need to do your own research, your own experiments, to see how they work, and the truth is that the more you know about crystals, the more effective they are. You may put them around plants so that they grow quicker, or you may want to put them on a photo and send healing energy (remember, where thought goes, energy flows), as quartz is an amplifier of energy.

Crystals are not magic, they are not of the occult, they are not to be feared and I am thankful that at last they are being used in many homes and workplaces. Choosing a crystal is easy, and once you have one it can be yours for life unless you are inspired to give it away, which is often the case. As there is now a good choice of books available, I have only included basic information here.

Crystals come from lava that has solidified, and depending on which cavity it lands in and what compound is there, it creates a particular crystal. It is similar to how we are made. If we have parents that originate from a certain part of the world, we will have certain features.

It was in the 1st century AD that people dedicated a stone to each month, thereby creating our birthstones which are still in use today, and the custom of wearing these stones became popular in the 18th century in Poland and then spread to the rest of Europe and on to rest of the world.

The Second World War relied on crystals too, as they ignited the bombs. On a lighter note, they are used today in surgery, computers, clocks and radios. Quartz watches, computers, televisions and many conventional medical techniques would not exist without crystals.

We base our entire measurement of time upon piezoelectric vibrations from quartz crystal. The scientific theory is that piezoelectric currents are tiny electrical charges that are produced when pressure is applied to a specific kind of crystal, and even lighters harvest the surge of piezoelectricity into a spark that ignites a flame.

Crystals and gemstones are surrounded by mythology, and throughout history there are many legends that mention crystals and their magical powers. We are all familiar with the idea of fortune-tellers gazing into crystal balls and foretelling the appearance of tall, dark strangers.

The ancient Greeks saw quartz and believed it to be frozen water because it was transparent, and so they gave it the name Crystallos. The earliest Papyrus mention of crystals dates back to 1600 BC, and the early Egyptians would crush Malachite and Lapis Lazuli to aid eye problems and produce eye make-up. Rubies were symbols of power and romance in the Middle Ages, and ladies often presented their knights with jewels to show their love.

The Bible mentions crystals more than 500 times, so for me, that rules out the problem many have with them being 'of the devil', which was often said when I began working with them. Thankfully, things have changed for the better and we no longer have banners outside shops or at shows. (Having said that, I did have a very scary time with a certain radical religious group when I opened my second shop, who literally threatened to hurt me and my family if I didn't close my business).

Choosing a crystal is easy, as all you need to do is let yourself be attracted to one. Some people believe the old wives' tale that a crystal should be bought for you, but I believe that this is just that – an old wives' tale. You may find that you are attracted to its colour or its shape.

If you find yourself in a shop full of crystals you'll be drawn to pick up a certain one, and once you do this you may find you don't want to put it down. Even if you do put it back, you will notice that as you browse around the shop you will want to return to it.

Often, people worry that if they're buying a crystal for a gift they may be attracted to it because they like it, but if you are choosing a crystal for another person, just think of that person and you'll be guided to the correct one.

Some people like to use a pendulum to choose a crystal. This simply means holding a pendulum over the selected crystals and dowsing for the correct one. Dowsing has been used for centuries to look for water, etc., but it is also a great way to choose a crystal.

For those of you who don't know how to use a pendulum, sit quietly holding the pendulum next to your heart chakra to get to know it and, when ready, hold the end of the chain and ask it to show you how it will swing when it wants to show yes to a question; then repeat for no and the same again to find not sure or don't know.

Using a pendulum is great fun and can be very helpful in finding objects, too. I recently found an old family grave, which had no marker, in an overgrown area of the graveyard. You can also check if food is okay to eat if you have allergies.

It can have many more uses, but please beware of getting addicted to it, as I've seen how some people will not make a decision without the pendulum saying they can.

> '*When man liberates his inner potential he becomes powerful and everything is possible*.' Bolivian Shaman Chamalu

There are many reasons why we cleanse crystals, such as the trauma of the crystal being mined, which may have included being extracted with the use of explosives or being cleansed in a bath of acid and transported many thousands of miles. They may already have changed hands several times and we have no idea how these people were feeling at the time.

The crystal may have absorbed some negative energy (but this does not mean being paranoid if someone touches your crystal). Just use your intuition and if you feel that the energy of a person who has touched your pendant is not so good, all you need to do is to 'clear' the item. Various ways of cleansing crystals include:

Soaking in a water solution. Variations on this include adding crab apple flower remedy. Some say sea salt can be used, but I find this is hard for certain crystals, so until you know more, keep it simple. Holding it under running water such as a stream or waterfall would have been used in early times, but is not always easy today.

✳ Burying them in the earth, but do remember where you buried them! This is a useful method when a crystal has been overworked and is well drained, or when it has taken on a lot of negativity.

✳ Placing in moonlight.

✳ Visualising light streaming through and 'washing' the crystal.

✳ Smudging with herbs or incense (natural).

✳ Using sound, either by chanting, placing in a singing bowl or directing some sort of sound through the crystal.

Practical considerations include avoiding hot water, as some crystals, for example Celestite, are very soft and fragile, and suit methods such as smudging rather than placing in water. There are no set rules as to how long the crystal should be cleansed for, but sense the energies emerging from the crystal and judge the amount of time by using this feeling or your intuition.

On the following pages are just a few of the most commonly known crystals and some *very basic* descriptions of their uses, as there are many more books available now on this subject.

Agate – Helps increase flexibility in one's life and in one's body and mind. It is an excellent stone for mathematical endeavours and can help one return from the depths of depression. It assists in the assimilation of zinc and vitamins A and D. Also used for disorders of the colon and digestive tract.

Amber – Exerts positive influence on endocrine system, spleen and heart. Healing, soothing, harmonising, it helps the body to heal itself by absorbing negative energy. It has been successful in the treatment of disorders of the throat, kidneys and bladder. It must be cleansed after each use, as it can absorb negative radiation.

Amethyst – Very good for any problems with sleep, and once in sleep it can help you to remember dreams. Good for headaches, migraines or depression, also useful for meditation and spiritual work. Can help with hormones, endocrine and metabolism, and it is becoming a well-known practice to place an amethyst with a deceased person to help their transition.

Aventurine – Good for reducing fevers and joint inflammation, and useful as an elixir for skin problems. Has a good effect on the lungs, heart and muscles, as well as helping the nervous system. Green Aventurine is known as the fortune stone. Blue is popular for communication issues, and excellent for meditation and connecting to your higher self.

Blue Lace Agate – A great stone to use for issues dealing with communication and creativity. When soaked in water for twelve hours and then gargled, it is good for sore throats. It has peaceful energies that can have a positive effect on the mind.

Bloodstone – As the name suggests, it is good for helping any problems with the blood. It is known as a good grounding stone. Also stimulates flow of lymph and metabolic processes. Ancient Egyptians used it to shrink tumours.

Calcite – Name gives a hint as to its uses. Calcite is good for teeth and bones. Stimulates blood clotting and is great for skin problems. Having this stone in your room will help clear negativity and keep the energies clear. Using this stone around your children, i.e. in the bedroom, could help their growth.

Carnelian – Energises the blood and helps kidneys, lungs, liver, gall bladder and the pancreas. Good for tissue regeneration and vitalises physical/emotional/mental bodies. Enhances attunement with inner self and also helps concentration.

Celestite – Enhances thyroid functions, reduces stress and can help one adjust to higher, more rarefied states of awareness, such as working with the Angelic realm. Also helps with clear speech, disorders of the eyes, ears, digestive system and intestines.

Chrysocolla – Treats arthritis, bone disease and muscle spasms. Good for lung problems and also female problems including PMS and cramps. It helps personal power and can increase creativity, as it reduces mental tension.

Citrine – Sometimes known as poor man's amber, its qualities help to bring abundance to the wearer/carrier. It is a great stone for stomach and liver problems and issues with poor self-esteem/confidence. It is one of the few stones that don't need clearing.

Clear Quartz – Is one of the most well-known and most used crystals, as it is an amplifier of energy and also absorbs, stores and releases energy; it also transmutes negativity. It's excellent for bringing clarity to the wearer/carrier and has many uses including healing broken bones and fractures, and is also excellent for spinal problems. A piece of quartz used in a glass of water and drunk daily can really help keep your energy high.

Garnet (Red) – Strengthens, purifies, vitalises and regenerates body systems, especially the bloodstream. Has strong affinity with root chakra, helping to harmonise the potent forces of the kundalini. It stimulates the pituitary gland, helps treat the spine and spine fluid, and enhances assimilation of iodine, calcium, magnesium and vitamins A, D and E.

Hematite – Good for all issues concerning blood. Helps flow of oxygen throughout the bloodstream and helps with anaemia. Cleanses kidneys and stimulates iron in the system. Good grounding stone and good to hold in a crisis. Care is needed during menstruation, as it can 'pull' the oxygen through the body.

Herkimer Diamond – Reduces stress, and balances and purifies energy within the body and mind. It has similar qualities to clear quartz. It increases awareness of dreams, hence it is known as the dream crystal. This stone is great to use as a spray to clear unwanted energies and also for helping areas with geopathic stress lines.

Jade – Green Jade is the most commonly known and has been used for centuries for its good luck properties, and if carried, it can bring good fortune. Good for healing lungs, kidneys and fertility problems, and if placed on the forehead it's said to help dream awareness.

Jasper – Great for stomach and liver problems, and it balances the mineral content within the body. The colour of the stone will show which area of the body can be treated, as each colour will have a different use (refer to chakra chart). Brown is a good grounding stone.

Kyanite – This is a great stone to have in your possession, as it helps to clear negativity from the Chakras and Aura and has a great effect on the system in general. This is another stone to help with transition, including death. Care is needed when carrying this stone, as it can be very sharp, so I would suggest keeping it wrapped or in a pouch.

Labradorite – This is a great stone to wear/carry, as it keeps energy high, balances the Chakras and helps keeps the Aura clear. It is useful for spinal problems too and can balance hormones, as well as help reduce blood pressure.

Lapis Lazuli – Alleviates pain, especially migraines. Good for throat, thyroid and parathyroid problems and has a good effect on third-eye activities, such as clear seeing.

Malachite – Good for relieving pain, especially menstrual and lung related. It can treat arthritis and swollen joints, and toothache. Known as the midwife stone, it helps with childbirth, as it eases labour. Care is needed with children and pets though, as it's toxic.

Moonstone – A stone of new beginnings, it's useful for most female problems whether they are physical, mental or emotional. Menopausal disorders, especially hot flushes, can be treated with this stone. Some women may need to remove this stone when there's a full moon.

Onyx – Relieves stress, balances male/female polarities, strengthens bone marrow and enhances emotional balance and self-control. It can help heal old hurts and works with Chakras according to the colour of the stone.

Black Onyx makes a great grounding stone.

Rose Quartz – Known as the love stone/stress stone. Placing it in the bedroom is said to attract love into your life and even holding it will help bring calm into your being. It can help a person to regain a sense of well-being. Good stone to use if finding it difficult to let go of something, be it emotional or mental. Great to use for lung, kidney and skin problems, and is especially good for fertility problems.

Topaz Gold – Good for tissue regeneration and the endocrine glands, and detoxifies the body. A warming, awakening, inspiring stone used to strengthen the liver, gallbladder, spleen, digestive organs and nervous system.

Tourmaline – Has electrical and magnetic properties when rubbed or heated. Comes in many colours and each works with the chakra it connects to, but in general, it's good for cleansing, purifying and transforming energies. Black Tourmaline is great for placing next to electrical equipment, especially computers and mobiles, as it transforms the low frequency coming from the equipment into energy.

One of the easiest ways to get to know the properties of crystals is to meditate with them. Simply sit with one and attune to its vibration. It's great for settling your body down and the longer you spend doing this the more benefits you will get. Each crystal you hold while you relax will give you a different experience, so experiment and enjoy finding out what these little beauties can do for you.

A good but simple reference point when using crystals on the body is to look at the chakra chart. Look at the problem part and then find the organ/gland nearest to it, then look for the colour of the chakra, find crystals of the same colour and lay them on the body. This is a great way to help the area that is out of balance.

Crystals can do many, many things, including:

* Redress imbalances in the energy system that might eventually lead to disorders in the body.

* Energise food and water. Placing clear quartz in food cupboards or in a glass used for drinking water helps to keep the body in a charged state. This is also great for those with back problems, as the energy of the crystal, which then charges the water that is drunk, in turn affects the nerve endings in the spinal column.

✳ Place them around electrical equipment or the home/car for calming.

✳ A great tool for meditation. Different crystals can help with different outcomes; trust your own intuition, always the best way and remember the possibilities are endless!

Crystals also vary their structure when they are subjected to changes in temperature and water levels (hydration), and they even change colour if you alter their electromagnetic field. We use this characteristic in order to see the black figures on the face of a quartz LCD watch.

Crystalline structures are everywhere, even in the human body where they are found on the surface of cells and in the cell 'battery', the mitochondria.

As during crystal healing the crystals are placed on the part of the body where the nerve clusters are found (usually around the chakra area), it's easy to understand how this could lead to significant alterations within the nervous system and affect the body's chemistry. Also, given that our emotions are governed by our chemistry, it stands to reason that crystals will affect our moods.

Crystal therapy is defined as the structured use of natural minerals obtained from the earth to achieve balance and harmony of the human mind, body and spirit. There hasn't been much scientific research into crystal therapy, but there is very strong evidence to suggest that people do feel better after a treatment. As with all forms of complementary medicine, it is vital to see a qualified crystal practitioner.

I believe that crystal therapy helps the client become aware of the reason for the complaint in their system; it gets to the root of the issue, rather than dealing with the effect, and because of this it often then works through and heals the rest of the system.

Clear quartz point:
Place your crystal in a glass of water and leave for at least 20 minutes to charge the water. The sun and the moon energise the crystal, which in turn energises the water, so that when you drink it, it goes into your system and helps you to release the blockages that have created the problem. It's good to keep it on the kitchen windowsill, so that each time you pass, you will drink and refill.

Also, you can place quartz in the bath as a bath remedy. The best time for this is the morning, as the life force is strongest with the rising sun. Cover as much of the body as possible as the aura is in constant motion and allows the water to penetrate the energy. Try to stay in the water for as long as possible, but for at least 15 minutes. Also lie down for a few minutes afterwards to help the blood re-circulate.

Self-healing technique:
1 medium milky/opaque crystal point (female) placed in left hand pointing up.
1 medium-sized clear quartz crystal point (male) placed in right hand pointing down.
1 small crystal female point above the head facing down.
1 clear cluster at the feet.
The larger the cluster used, the greater the force field.

Clear Quartz = masculine or positive, and when introduced into your electromagnetic field this quartz restores low or weakened energy levels.
Milky or Opaque Quartz = feminine or negative. These energies are calming and will reduce tension caused by over-activity.
Two of each type is needed to ensure the balance of Yin and Yang energies throughout the self healing.
In crystal therapy, the quartz crystal has the role of receiver and transmitter of healing energies and using equal amounts of male and female quartz crystals during self-healing, aims to restore the body's overall balance and harmony.

Back problems:
Lie down in a comfortable position (with something under your knees if you need to) and have soft music playing in the background. Using five citrine tumble-stones (for calming the nervous system), place one stone below the feet, one each side of the knees and one each side of the elbow area.
Place an amethyst in the centre of the forehead, a quartz at the base of the spine and another at the base of the skull. Allow yourself to remain in this relaxed state for twenty minutes or so, unless your intuition tells you to remove the crystals sooner.
The spine not only supports your back, but is the centre of your nervous

system and where your chakras are positioned. Back pain can be caused by a number of things, so if the problems persist, always seek advice from a medical doctor.

Chakra balance:

1. At the root chakra, check with a pendulum to see if the chakra is blocked, unbalanced or excessive.

2. Work your way up to the crown, placing a quartz tumble on each chakra to clear it of negativity. Leave for around 20 minutes while relaxing with soft music. Relaxation music is important, as it helps you un-clutter your mind while the crystals do their work.

3. As you take the clear crystal off, replace it with a coloured stone according to the colour of the chakra. Thank the crystals as you take them off (always show respect to the elements) and leave for around 20 minutes while you relax.

4. Balance the chakras two at a time by holding your hands above them, until all done.

5. Take off from the crown and thank each one, going down to the root.

6. Stroke aura downwards from either side, and if you can't reach, just imagine it to be and it is done.

Depression and headaches:

Crystals help you reach the centre of the problem, helping you understand why the pain is there. Lie down, begin to breathe slowly and have peaceful music playing in the background. Place an amethyst on your throat, a smoky quartz on your forehead and a clear quartz above your head, and focus on the words 'release' and 'peace'.

You'll find the problem often comes to the fore with an understanding of why the tension is with you. By understanding why it has come into your system, you can often deal with the problem and release the situation.

Room clearing:

Use the pendulum to find out where the negative spots are in the room. Once you have located one, place the quartz cluster in the area and leave overnight. Clear the crystal as advised, and then work around the rest of the room(s).

Always cleanse the crystals when finished.

Double termination crystals:

These crystals have a point at each end, sometimes artificially. This makes it a very strong crystal to use, as the energy flows in both directions. These crystals are great for healing, as they absorb negativity and break old patterns.

Taking care of your crystals:

When the moon is full, place them in the window-sill to clear any negative energy and when the sun is shining, place them in the window to energise your crystals. This way you will get what the crystals have to offer for longer.

Always remember, the intention is very important when working with crystals.
Just relax, knowing there is no wrong way to do it.

Chapter 12

Reiki

'*Before practising healing others, it is necessary to heal your own life to bring stability into your own life.*' – Dr Usui

REIKI is the ancient art of healing by touch.

The most acceptable meaning of the word 'Rei' is universal, 'Ki' is life force, and so by combining Rei and Ki we get universal life force. I believe this is a good definition of the word Reiki.

I think of Reiki as a 'spiritual drain cleaner', which unblocks any negative emotions that have been trapped (usually unknowingly). Regular use of Reiki can promote love and harmony within, which then has an effect on those around us.

Ki flows through all living things, and as long as something is alive it has Ki flowing through it.

Ki has been given many different names by each culture, all referring to the same thing – energy.

Chinese = Chi
Hawaiian = Mana
Sanskrit/Hindu = Prana
Christians = Light or Holy Ghost
Jewish Cabalists = Jesod
Sioux = Wakan

Reiki is another useful tool for self-awareness/personal growth and can also help us release issues from the past. It's becoming a very popular therapy, and whereas a few years ago no one would dare say they were having a treatment, today, even people in nursing professions are receiving Reiki attunements to help them with their work.

Reiki brings about change in your life and many people who've had this therapy, or had their Reiki attunements, say their life has changed for the better. When having a treatment you might find things that have been held inside for a very long time now have a way of working through to the surface, enabling you to resolve them. After all, it's the letting go of old issues that seems to be most difficult.

Reiki is a way of channelling energy to not only address physical disorders, but also to open the mind to the causes of dis-ease and pain. Remember, our body is talking to us all the time, trying to give us messages about something, usually something that isn't flowing in our life.

This consciousness of the Higher Self, or God-force, is by definition all knowing. It understands each individual completely, knows the cause of the problem being faced and what to do to heal it. The fact is, people actually heal themselves!

'*Curving back within myself I create again and again.*' Bhagavad Gita, Sacred Sanskrit Text

In a Reiki treatment the practitioner places their hands in a number of positions over the client's body, thereby acting as a channel or conductor for Reiki energy. Or, if the practitioner has received Reiki 11, they may find that hands are not placed directly on the body, as they work in the energy field.

The energy begins to move through the client's system, naturally directing itself to the source of imbalance. Consequently, the outcome of each individual treatment is different, since it is determined not by the practitioner but by the system of the person receiving the treatment, as the intention sets the outcome.

After treatment, some people experience what are known as contraindications, which can include runny noses, visiting the toilet more often, wanting to cry or, in some cases, wanting to release anger. These symptoms and others may occur as the body begins to release what is no longer needed, including toxins.

Reiki is a powerful tool for change and those who go on to become attuned to Reiki, or become a practitioner, see great changes in their life. An attunement/initiation is where a Reiki Master brings symbols into the chakra system, to bring in certain vibrations so that you can self-heal or to carry out the treatments on other life forms, such as animals, plants and minerals.

An initiation suggests the start of something new and that's what it is;

it's a way of seeing and feeling life in a new way. Reiki is a special kind of life force that is activated once the person has had the attunement. The symbols placed in the system are an ancient language that holds its own vibration, so to have that symbol in your own vibration will indeed alter it.

It takes around three to four weeks for some people to adjust to the Reiki 1 attunement, and symptoms of a clear-out can occur. That's why it's important to carry out self-healing daily, as it helps the clearing and also keeps the energy activated and flowing freely. These attunements clear the channels to allow the energy to flow and once this is done they will remain open for the rest of the person's life.

Many convey a feeling of having a closer relationship with nature after an attunement and say they see life more clearly. But do not confuse this with never having to clear your system again, or never having another illness. We each have our own journey to make, and when there's an issue you don't want to deal with, you will block it out just like anyone else. The advantage of having the knowledge of Reiki and the ability to remove problems from the system, means that you can follow your body language and look at events from a whole-istic point of view.

The attunement of Reiki 11 increases the level of healing energy within the mental, emotional and karmic layers, and after this attunement, old issues and emotions usually resurface to be released. This is often where many wished they'd never bothered, as old wounds return and can be rather painful. But again, it's better out than in!

Also, Reiki 11 brings in the ability to do distant healing and great results can be achieved, although there's a little controversy about what happens when we send healing without the person giving consent. But I believe that nothing is wasted and if you send healing to a person who doesn't know about it and they do not want it, it will simply return; unless you set the intension to go elsewhere if not received (I usually set the intension to go to the planet if not received).

Reiki 111 is the Master's degree and a Master is simply one who has mastered a discipline, so let's not let the ego get carried away with the title!

I recently came across Essential Reiki by Diane Stein, which I imagine has caused a lot of controversy in the world of Reiki, as she seems to go against many of the rules by teaching in a more relaxed manner. I must say, I do agree with her values though, as I believe it's a system that can help change the world for the better.

> *'Affluence, unboundedness and abundance are our natural states; we need only to recapture what we already know.'* Deepak Chopra

Reiki is not a religion, as it holds no creeds or doctrine. A belief in God is not needed, only a belief in love. Different variations in this energy system exist, but try not to get caught up in the politics, just enjoy having this wonderful energy, as it is a blessing to us all. Reiki has five principles to follow:

1. Just for today, do not worry.
2. Just for today, do not anger.
3. Honour your parents, teachers and elders.
4. Earn your living honestly.
5. Show gratitude to every living thing.

Reiki is not sent by the practitioner to the healer, but is drawn through the body of the healer from universal energy. The energy moves through the purified channel within the healer, thus ensuring that they never pass any of their personal energy field on to the recipient. As a consequence, the therapist is never drained when giving healing, because they too are treated in the process of giving treatment.

When seeking Reiki attunements, try to have a treatment from the Reiki Master first, as this will allow you to have a good rapport with this person and, as always, trust your intuition. Don't push it either, as I have heard about someone wanting the treatment or attunement done by a certain date, but they find that something goes wrong with the appointment. You'll find that this could be a message from your higher self to postpone the appointment, as it's not the correct time or the right person doing the treatment.

Reiki is a gentle treatment which I enjoy giving and receiving, and I am most privileged to be able to attune others for their healing process to begin, and as it's now become a common therapy, I'm sure Dr Usui is pleased with its popularity.

> *'Talking, thinking, arguing, hoping and praying for a better life only satisfy a superficial level of the mind, and hardly that. When real change occurs, it is real; it is not a mood. It has nothing with keeping wary over your problems or trying your best to control your impulses. They are your reality.'* Deepak Chopra

Chapter 13

Healing

THERE HAS ALWAYS been a battle between health and disease, as disease was on the earth long before man, as fossils show. But efforts to combat disease became very technical, and natural healing had to take a back seat. Thankfully, things are changing for the better and healing is making a comeback, although more slowly than I would like for certain practices such as crystal therapy, especially when we have evidence that quartz is an amplifier of energy and that we can accept it as such an important part of our daily lives.

Healing simply means 'to make whole' and has a recorded history of over 4,000 years; therefore, how can the medical profession not accept that the whole personality needs considering, instead of repairing the damaged part. Healing involves a transfer of energy, which is what a doctor will help us with, although unlike a healer, he probably transfers knowledge rather than energy to stimulate the self-repair mechanism within the person.

Hippocrates (physician born 480 BC) believed that nature has its own healing force, and the Chinese, like Hippocrates, stressed the importance of studying the patient and would then work mainly with herbs, diet and acupuncture to produce a state of balance. Indian medicine was also widely established by the 8th century, and used minerals and precious stones for healing.

Millions of pounds have been spent on finding cures for illnesses, yet this figure is still growing and new diseases keep appearing, while the side effects of the drugs being administered are frightening. I realise they are given in good faith, but we have to realise that a drug isn't always the answer. We must begin to work together on this and allow patients to have access to therapies that can re-balance their energy, and this can be beneficial all round.

'The light of the body is the eye; therefore when thine eye is single, the whole body is full of light.' Jesus of Nazareth

People could be taught meditation and it could be made a part of our children's learning; then perhaps they wouldn't slump in a chair and fall asleep after a day at school. I am saddened by the amount of homework they have to do after a day at school too, and between school and the rules they must live by away from school, it's as if we don't want them to enjoy life.

Thankfully, things are starting to change for the better. The Doctor–Healer Network was founded in the UK in 1988 by a group of doctors who were working with healers to promote healing within the NHS. I was so excited when I heard about this, as it shows how far we have come since I was laughed at for wanting to open a shop that sold crystals. However, I think we still have a long way to go, as recently, I tried to open doors for Crystal Therapy within the workplace, but the doors were firmly shut tight. Yet, this makes me smile, as we rely on quartz for so much of our technology, including in hospitals. Even Reiki is being used, yet it's an energy-based treatment, whereas crystal can be scientifically proven. How strange!

Meditation:

Meditation is important; it brings calm to the body, lowers blood pressure and feels good when we have done it. Why, then, is it such a chore? I have included the section below because when I read it I remember disagreeing with him:

TAKEN FROM *THE PASSIONATE MIND* by Joel Kramer

One of the problems in these discussions is that it is extremely difficult to listen, whether it be to this person or to anyone else. Ordinarily what we do when we think we are listening is to take in the words, translate them into something that we know or are familiar with, and then agree or disagree. If the words fit our structure, our beliefs, the things we are comfortable with, the things we know, then the speaker is a wise man and we agree.

If the words do not please us, do not fit our structures and beliefs, do not give us pleasure, then the speaker is not a wise man and we disagree. That's what most of us do and we call it listening, for to listen there must be openness, and innocence, a putting away of the old ideas, so that possibly the fresh can come in. If you are busy involved in either agreeing or disagreeing (and you can watch yourself do this as you listen) then what you are doing is not listening at all and the new, which is the front of growth and learning, does not come in.

'I don't do that,' was *my* first reaction; was it yours?

No one wants to believe they can't listen, do they?

We like to believe that if anyone has a problem we can give them our undivided attention, but not too many people can, as our thoughts often drift off to another subject or time while we are listening, or we are waiting to give them our view before we forget what we want to say.

So if this can happen when we are trying to help a friend in need, it's understandable why a lot of people have trouble focusing on an unseen 'force' that wants to communicate with them.

In meditation, just as with listening to a friend's problems, it involves listening. This means listening to that small voice inside the self that wants us to be happy. Yet, this is one of the things I still have the most problems with.

When you are in a light level of sleep you are in the alpha range, which is 7 to 14 cycles per second, and going to the alpha level is essentially the same thing as meditating. When someone meditates, scientifically, they are simply reducing their brain wave frequency to alpha. The alpha level is the level we use to activate our minds.

This is no different to training your physical body to get into shape and training your mind to do the same. If you exercise your body only once per month you will get very different results than if you exercise daily. The same principle applies when you train and exercise your mind. The more you go into alpha, learn to visualise, relax and tune into your intuition, the healthier and better your life becomes.

> '*We simply act as our level of consciousness dictates. If we want to change our existence meaningfully, then we must change our level of consciousness.*' Deepak Chopra

According to Joan Borysenko PhD, a pioneer in the field of mind/body medicine, meditation can be broadly defined as any activity that keeps the attention pleasantly anchored in the present moment. When the mind is calm and focused in the present, it is neither reacting to memories from the pas nor being preoccupied with plans for the future, two major sources of chronic stress known to impact on health.

Experience in meditation comes with time and practice. Despite the resistance of the mind and the ego, it does not take long to experience that pleasant shift from outward to inward focus. Anyone can learn to meditate simply by practising, but the ego and conscious mind resists letting go. Many exercises are available for this important act, but many people find it hard to make the time to meditate and yet, when they do they find it so beneficial.

Another problem I had was trying to work out why we have to meditate all the time to keep our energy high, but over time I started to realise it has more to do with being on the right 'station' to seek advice or guidance. I now believe the most important thing is just about being ... then a natural progression will occur.

> 'Each day beckons you to walk on the road of self-transcendence. When we transcend ourselves, we do not compete with others, we compete only with our previous achievements. And each time we surpass our achievements, we get joy. Life is nothing but a perpetual possibility.' Sri Chinmoy, Indian Philosopher and Guru

Many people have trouble meditating because they cannot stop random thoughts whirling around in their head (also known as monkey chatter). It seems easy to just breathe and relax, but then the thoughts come: 'What if...'. The ego is very clever at taking us out of the moment and to the 'what ifs...' of our life. It is said that the ego is scared of peace, so it distracts us when we are trying to bring calm into our lives.

With the continued practice of meditation you can discover a greater sense of purpose and strength of will, and your thinking becomes clearer. When the mind is filled with the feeling of peace, it cannot take off on its own and worry, stress out or become depressed.

Anyone who practises enough can come to achieve this art, but discipline is needed just to do it regularly. Once you practise regularly, the benefits are great, and a shift from outward to inward focus comes with ease.

Here is a suggestion for starting to meditate.

Sit on a straight-backed chair or lie down, but try to keep your spine straight, as this is important for the flow of energy. Make sure you will not be disturbed for at least 10–15 minutes to start with (eventually increasing to around 30 minutes) and relax your body by breathing slowly and evenly, counting your breaths, three in and three out.

Keep repeating this for a few minutes, be aware of your body and feel how relaxed it is. Starting at the bottom, relax your toes, feet, calves, knees, thighs and then relax your lower body, all your internal organs. Follow this with your upper body, arms and hands, then your neck and your jaw, relax your eyes and finish by relaxing your mind.

Notice how you feel now and continue with the slow breathing and slow thoughts.

If this is done once or twice a week, it will show good results.

For a long time I wondered if I was 'doing it right', and I would look at the people in the group I was in who would say:

'I saw light doing this or that.'

Many would talk of a great journey they'd been on while meditating and I would feel useless, as I hadn't 'been anywhere'. I later found that some people would make up an experience to feel part of the group.

Take your time and find the way that feels right for you. There's no rush, it's not a race, and as everything is as it should be, the time will be right when you have your own truth, brought to you by you!

There are some beautiful guided meditations around today. In the past, I found guided meditations or journeys easier, as they allowed my mind to think that it's doing something, unlike what I term 'blank mind' meditation.

So look for something that appeals to your language and your mindset. But I would like to recommend the Divinity Publishing series, as these are beautiful and very easy to follow; I have often used them and recommended them to customers.

Another simple way to meditate is to candle gaze, where you sit comfortably without interruption and gaze at the flame of a candle. While looking into the flame, you find that chattering thoughts cease as you wonder at the beauty of the flame, and often your own insights will come to you.

Some of the wonderful benefits of regular meditation include:

* Drop in cholesterol level.
* Improved flow of air to the lungs resulting in easier breathing.
* Decrease in the ageing process.
* Greater creativity.
* Decreased anxiety and depression.
* Improved learning ability and memory.
* Increased feelings of vitality, happiness and joy

According to many people, one simple way to bring awareness into your life is through walking meditation. When we walk, we are usually absorbed in our thoughts to one extent or another. We are hardly ever in the moment and just walking. To do this exercise, focus your attention on each foot as it comes into contact with the ground.

When the mind wanders away from the feet or legs, or the feeling of the body walking, re-focus your attention. Don't look around, but keep your gaze in front of you. This brings your attention to the actual experience of walking as you are doing it, as you are focusing on the sensations in your feet and legs, and feeling your whole body moving.

> '*Always remember that seclusion is the price of greatness. Walk in silence; go quietly; develop spirituality. We should not allow noise and sensory activities to ruin the antennae of our attention, because we are listening for the footsteps of God to come into our temples.*'
> Paramahansa Yogananda, Indian Yogi and Guru

If we carried out this information and meditated on a regular basis, it would truly make us 'magicians', as we would be able to bring in pure energy straight through the system. If we allowed the energy through, with no blocks in our system (as our chakras hold our total sum of thoughts, emotions and beliefs), then we could manifest the life we want *right now*.

Can you think of a time when there was something you wanted and all of a sudden it was there in your life? If so, you were probably in balance with your life at the time, with no blockages. I believe that is how Jesus managed the miracles he performed. He was in balance/harmony with himself and why he was here, and this is an example of how this can be achieved.

Sound:

Music can have a great effect on the spirit. Pythagoras called this form of healing 'musical medicine'. In Rome, physicians used Bach for digestion problems, Handel for grief and Schubert for insomnia, and we all know that Achilles 'played the lyre and sang away his anger'.

I hadn't made the connection to how important sound is to us until I met a man called Jeff Moran, who facilitated a workshop on angels and chakras and introduced us to sound by showing us how it actually changes matter. I couldn't get my head around this at first, but then he explained how the voice itself is a powerful tool in the healing process as sound changes matter, as demonstrated when a soprano shatters glass when she sings.

He also demonstrated the effect of sound and vibration with Tibetan singing bowls and used one made of quartz crystal (which amplifies sound). This was an awesome experience, as it filled the entire room with a loud humming sound and we could actually feel the waves of energy; a friend of mine had just finished work and had a headache, and this method cleared it within minutes.

I suppose it shouldn't be so hard to believe that sound can help to bring the body back into alignment; after all, if each chakra resonates to a specific note on the musical scale, then it stands to reason that we can use it for healing. Also, the human body is composed of many crystalline substances, and when these structures of the body become heavy or too dense they can't function properly and certain sounds will re-balance it.

As our bodies are 70% water, that makes them excellent conductors for sound and vibration, and as we don't just hear with our ears but literally feel the vibrations with every cell in our body, it's understandable that noises such as someone yelling or shouting abuse at us is going to have a negative effect on our system. It literally depresses us, which will affect the immune system, which can eventually lead to dis-ease.

Even before we're born, music makes a difference, as hearing is the first sense to develop. The unborn child will be affected by what it hears for at least half the pregnancy. Researchers have found that making and even hearing certain sounds can have a neurophysiologic effect on the brain, and the type of music played will play an important role in our health.

If you play music that has a really heavy beat, it will affect the base chakra and therefore, the mood of the person isn't exactly going to be relaxed, is it? Beethoven is good grounding music. Angel-style music is good for working with our intuition and healing, etc., and many scientists, musicians, doctors and health practitioners now refer to the undisputed power of sound as preventative, restorative and advanced promotive of health and healing.

'We know that sound and music have profound effects on the immune system, which clearly does have a lot to do with the remission of cancer,' quotes Dr Mitchell Gaynor, Molecular Biologist Director at New York's Strang Cancer Prevention Center.

For years, Dr Gaynor has run a free support group by beginning the session with meditation, accompanied by him playing 'singing bowls'.

How wonderful!

A practice I would love to see here one day!

Hypnotherapy:

The term hypnotism was invented by a contemporary of John Elliotson, James Braid (1795–1860), who spent much of his life as a general physician and surgeon in Manchester, England.

Hypnotherapy is a great way to look at some of our fears and bad habits that we can't manage to shake off. It's also great for relieving physical pain, including emotional and mental, but sadly, many people are led to believe that to be hypnotised is to be 'put under' and that after the session they will be told everything that has happened, as we're all familiar with the stage routines that we've been entertained by.

In fact, it is nothing like that!

These are very gentle therapies which take you to a very relaxed place, and once there your conscious mind can be distracted while your subconscious mind can recall events that are buried deep within your memory cells. The client does the talking and the recalling, the therapist just facilitates the event and takes notes, etc.

My first encounter with hypnosis was through a session of past life regression. I was rather wary and very cynical, but curious all the same. When relaxed and in a meditative state I knew I was talking to the man facilitating the session, but at the same time there was a scene going on in my head showing me something else.

The feelings, smells and sense of being there were strange, to say the least.

Regression:

Regression is going back to a specific time and healing how we feel about it, and also how we can change our view of it. To be regressed means going back to the memory that's stored in your consciousness; for instance, if I asked you to think back to last Christmas and how you spent it.

If I played music at the same time as asking, you would probably remember where you were, who you were with, what you were wearing and also what you ate. If you were deeply relaxed while remembering it, you could probably smell the food or, in some situations, even taste it.

Just sit for a few moments and remember what you were doing and who was there. What did the food smell like, taste like? Was there music playing? Or were you watching TV? See how easy it is? And you haven't even left your chair.

Don't worry if you find this exercise emotional, as reliving these memories often taps into emotions that are waiting to be released. It's your mind, your consciousness, that is bringing this information up and you can do that as far back as you want to, but I believe this work is best done with a reputable therapist; some people may not be able to deal with certain events that spring up.

Emotions can be carried forward, even emotions from past lives, such as the feelings of love and loss, bitterness and power struggles. Also, sometimes we may have had a traumatic or fearful death in another life and may have brought that fear into this life, or we could have been a very cruel person and we may take the guilt with us into our 'death'.

Being a bad person in another life always seems to be difficult to accept. No one wants to believe they have been a baddie; we all like to think we have been a very nice person, and some people want to be someone famous.

Certain events from past lives can sometimes present themselves as physical birthmarks, physical pain or a disability in this life, and past life regression helps to uncover much deeper issues. It can help us see both sides of a situation.

> *'The seed you sow today will not produce crop till tomorrow. For this reason, your identity does not lie in your current results. This is not who you are ... your current results are who you were.'*
>
> James Arthur Ray

It's said that if you are a victim in this life, you were possibly a person who misused your power in a previous incarnation. This in turn may help you learn how to manage your present situation. I know this was certainly true in my own situation.

Past lives have come to be seen as a tool for personal development, to learn the lessons of complex relationships, access guidance from your higher self or reveal your life purpose. *Many Lives, Many Masters* by Brian Weiss is a very good book to read, as is *Through Time Into Healing*, but my personal favourite is *Only Love is Real*. I think his books are great to read, but I also believe Dr Weiss is taken a little more seriously due to the fact that he is a 'real' doctor.

Past lives can also help us to make more sense of our lives when it comes to personal tragedy, such as losing a baby, etc. Some people ask how they'll know the difference between whether they had a genuine past life experience or made it all up. You will know because you will always remember each detail and this will never change, no matter how many times you tell the tale.

There were references to reincarnation (to reincarnate) in the Old and New Testaments of the Bible, but in AD 325 the Roman Emperor Constantine the Great, along with his mother Helen, deleted references contained in the New Testament, and in AD 553 the Second Council of Constantinople confirmed this action and said that the idea of reincarnation was heresy.

Yet, the early church fathers accepted that reincarnation was real and many, including the early Gnostics, believed they had lived before and would again, and many of the ancient teachings believed in reincarnation.

Scientists are now beginning to seek answers to some of the questions that Past Life Regression (PLR) presents us with and we have a lot to gain from this research, as it will finally be taken seriously. Research into the mysteries of the mind and soul continuation will show how these experiences affect our present behaviour.

There are thousands of cases recorded scientifically, many of which involve children who are speaking in a foreign language to which they would have no access or birthmarks in the same spot they'd been wounded in a previous life. There are even stories of children who could take you to a family they once belonged to in a previous life and could tell you all their names and the details of who they were when they were alive.

'*The secret of happiness is not in doing what one likes, but in liking what one does.*' J. M. Barrie, Scottish Author

Many people find that after a therapy they have the confidence to do things they've always dreamt of, such as sailing or flying, as they will have cleared something that has been stuck in their subconscious for a long time, possibly lifetimes.

My first taste of PLR made the relationships I'd had in my life make so much sense; even more so over the next few years, as more snippets would surface. I remembered watching a scene on TV one day and somehow I knew that 'I' was like the man on the screen. More spooky was that one day at work I frightened my daughter and she literally froze on the spot as I rushed into the room in a bad mood, and somehow, I felt her fear and knew it was because of me. I asked her what the problem was and she told me she'd 'backtracked' to a lifetime that we'd had together. She confirmed what I had begun to believe, that I had indeed been a very violent man in that lifetime.

Thankfully, we were in a healthy situation and so were able to discuss such things, and this has helped us come to an understanding, as you can imagine the guilt I felt knowing I'd hurt my daughter, even though she wasn't my daughter then. It would have been devastating to find out what I did and not be able to talk openly about it with her, and that's why it's so important to seek a genuine practitioner.

We've spent time talking over her feelings too, as she remembered why so many times throughout her life she had felt scared of me, although I've never raised a hand to her in this life. More than that though, she's been my rock, as it would have been so much harder to bear without being able to discuss it with her.

Also, we've since trained together to become PLR practitioners, as we both know how important this therapy is to healing emotional/physical and mental wounds in this life. Because she's helped me come to terms with the abuse I put her through in the former life, it's helped me to forgive myself, and more so, to forgive the men who have hurt me in this life. I suppose it's a way of seeing both sides of the coin; after all, I cannot judge another person for violence when I know I have walked in those same shoes.

'*Every grain of sap contains the full value of the whole tree.*'
Maharishi Mahesh Yogi, Founder of Transcendental
Meditation

While going through the stages of forgiving myself (or previous self) my daughter taught me to realise that we can only love to the best of our ability, given the situation we are in at any one given moment. She is very wise for her years – always has been – and will make a fantastic doctor of psychology.

I now realise we can only use what we have at the time, and often what most of us are working from is fear. A person who inflicts pain on any life form can only be working from fear, and any emotion that is not love is fear; they are the two polarities of the heart. Even if we are acting out of hurt, grief or resentment, etc., it's really fear, as any emotion can be taken back to its core, and it will be fear if it is not love.

CHAPTER 14

More Energy Tools

ANGELS:

I decided to include this subject, as I have been privileged on more than one occasion to experience angelic energy over the years. At first, I thought I'd never tell anyone in case they thought me mad, but I really feel the need to share the fact that there is a very powerful band of energy that we call angels just waiting to help us, whenever we call, usually in our darkest moments.

A young man said to me one day that he wished he had a belief or a sign that someone was guiding him. I thought how sad it was that this youngster didn't know that there is a guiding force to be used whenever he wishes. Then I remembered that I used to be there; I'd forgotten that I used to be in the dark place of not believing in a force to tap into.

> *'We can't see the wind — we can only see its effect — it's the same with thought.'* Marie Cunningham

When I had problems believing that angels could be real, I found that thinking of them as energy or vibration rather than a winged being helped. Angel is from the Greek word Angelos meaning messenger, and messengers come in many forms, including humans and animals. In this section, the angels referred to are the religious angels from history. There are millions everywhere, and just like humans, not one is identical to another.

They have personalities and attributes of their own that they can use to help us when we ask. They embody the power, wisdom and love of GOD/ SOURCE. They are omnipresent (they can be in more than one place at a time) and as they have no time or space we shouldn't worry we are taking them away from someone/something when we ask for their help.

Guides, fairies, elementals, nature spirits and divas are part of an energy stream just as angels are, but they are working on different vibrations. I think of it as a little like the radio station having more than one band with lots of stations on each one.

When our higher self/soul makes the decision to be born, a Guardian Angel is there. Thus, from the moment our incarnation (life) is planned, we are accompanied by this being that will be with us at our physical birth, and will accompany us through life and eventually death. It will not interfere with our free will, but will travel with us and, when possible, protect us if we are in danger and will witness our joy and comfort our tears.

Many children are aware of their Guardian Angel, but many lose that awareness as they get older (usually around the age of seven). This is said to be due to the awakening of the second chakra at that age, but is mainly due to parents and others telling them not to be silly if they report seeing such things. I find it strange that some adults and religious groups say they don't exist and yet there are so many pictures, statues and even hymns about them throughout history. The idea for these artefacts has to have come from somewhere.

If you have seen the film *City of Angels*, you will have noticed how the guardians watch what the humans do. Most of us watch the film and wonder why they don't step in before tragic events happen (just as I did with my house fire), but they cannot interfere, as we have free will and our journey is ours.

This seems a harsh reality, as today, human suffering and terror is at its height, but I believe life's like a movie and that we're all part of it, each having our part to play.

This still doesn't take away the fact that if anything unfortunate happens to myself or my family and friends that I myself don't 'go under' just as anyone else does.

> *'Just when I thought I had a handle on life, the handle broke.'*
> Mother Teresa

A lot of people get confused with this issue; they think that because I teach this subject I shouldn't be affected when someone I love dies, etc., and they wonder why I go to pieces. Be aware of the words I use, especially where I have highlighted them with quotation marks. My life, like everyone else's, is to have experiences and emotions, whatever they may be, and at such times when I'm in pain I'll do what most people do — I'll ask, 'Why me'?

Again, you may come across different information than what you are about to read, as there are many books available on this subject. There are said to be three realms of angels, each divided into three degrees. The first realm, closest to the divine, is Heavenly Counsellors, followed by Heavenly Governors and then Messengers.

HEAVENLY COUNSELLORS:

Seraphim. The word Seraphim means the inflamer and holds the highest rank in the angelic army. They conduct the music of the spheres and keep the right balance of sound and alignment of movement between the planets and other heavenly bodies.

Cherubim. The guardians of light, particularly that which comes from the stars, they enable mystical experiences and spread the perfect light of God in the form of love.

Thrones. These oversee the life of each of the planets. The major angel of the earth is a throne, but the moon also has a throne, as do Jupiter, Venus and so on. It is also said that the Virgin Mary is a throne.

HEAVENLY GOVERNORS:

Dominions. They will give advice, support and counsel to the lower groups.

Virtues. Sometimes known as the shining ones, they help respond to prayer and request for healing by focusing suitable concentration for divine energy into specific areas for specific individuals.

Powers. They look after the keeping of the Akashic records, inspire human conscience and oversee the rhythms of birth and death. I wonder if that is where the term 'the powers that be' comes from when we call for help.

MESSENGERS:

Principalities. They give guardianship to the nations, large groups and cities (got their job cut out there!). Maybe that's why we call school overseers 'principals'.

Archangels. These are the ones that help us to interpret divine principles. They overlook all aspects of human endeavour. The most commonly known archangels are Michael, Gabriel, Uriel and Raphael.

Michael means 'who is like the divine'. He is the guardian of the North, night-time, the season of winter, the element air, and our spirits and dreams. The colour blue helps us link to him. He is often seen as yielding a sword to ward off evil. He is about living in peace with others and is a protector.

Uriel means 'light and fire of the divine'. Guardian of the East, rising sun, the morning, spring, alchemy, the mind and the element of fire. Links through purple and gold, and lights the world of science, economics, politics and medical research. He helps us find direction in life.

Gabriel means 'divine is my strength'. Guardian of South, noon, summer, water and our emotions. He links with white. He is the one who told Mary she was pregnant. A protector of women and children, and can help dysfunctional families.

Raphael means 'the divine has healed'. Guardian of the West, twilight, evening, autumn, healing and the elements of earth. He links with green and growth, transformation and all forms of healing, from surgery to herbalists.

There are millions of angels helping in so many ways.

Angels, including Guardian Angels and Guiding Angels, protect and inspire us at very direct and personal levels. Your guiding angel will change as you change in the experiences and lessons that need to be learnt, and some people have a few working with them at one time.

When we understand more about the areas of expertise, we can invoke them to bring blessings, safety and protection. All we need to do is ask.

Many people start looking for proof of angels by asking for a white feather. This is often referred to as the calling card of the angels. They do not mind how many times you tell yourself the birds are moulting, or how it was brought in by your shoe and so on. I spent a long time making excuses after white fluffy feathers seemed to appear from nowhere.

When you are ready to ask for real help (although many people have trouble praying, through childhood programming) your angel can be contacted. It will be like picking up the phone and ringing a friend for a chat, although they tend not to chat.

Guides can 'talk' for longer, but angel talk is very brief and they tend to communicate in different ways, probably because they come from a different vibration. They can remove fear from your heart, make you aware of a colour or cause a gift to come your way.

'Space and silence are necessary because it is only when the mind is alone, uninfluenced, untrained, not held by infinite varieties of experience, that it can come upon something totally new.'
J. Krishnamurti, Spiritual Writer and Speaker

Invocation and meditation are important for stillness, making it easier for us to be aware of their presence. We usually busy ourselves with things that 'need' doing rather than sit in quiet contemplation. We are a crazy bunch of humans, and sometimes I think the angels must despair, although I'm told they don't, as they have no judgment.

Although many have male names, they are beyond gender, but they use their masculine/feminine qualities, which are perfectly balanced, when needed. The name you use isn't really that important, it's the intentions that is; and remember it is a vibration we are calling.

As with friends and family we need to keep in regular contact, have pictures around us and learn to listen to their guidance. Many people get confused between guides and angels. Guides watch over us, advise us and help us. They build a bridge for us between the different planes of reality, enabling us to acquire a greater understanding of life. They may be there mainly as personal companions, or they may require our help in fulfilling a broader mission to collective humanity.

Guides have different main areas of interest or expertise. If their mission to humanity is wide, they will focus on teaching, healing and inspiration, aiding research, helping interplanetary communication or any combination of these.

At a soul level we belong to families and groups. It's said that our guides are usually from within our soul group and we will have met them in previous incarnations. This is a subject that I have seen discussed often and with no agreement at the end.

Guides do not see each other as Native American Indians, etc., that's only for our purpose to help us recognise them and so that we are not too afraid by seeing something that we feel comfortable or at ease with. After all, if they showed themselves as an ET, they would frighten us and we would probably not want to see them again.

Communication with guides is usually done with thought waves or vibration, as they have no need for personality, etc. Accepting they are there to help is one thing, learning to recognise and use this help is another. People in meditation, healing or spiritual groups are usually taught how to communicate with their guides, but it can also be done at home, alone.

There is no proof they are there, and for those who do see them, they are usually there one minute and gone the next. There are many who have had experienced guides and angels, yet dare not speak of the experience.

> *'Faith is to believe what you do not yet see; the reward for this faith is to see what you believe.'* Saint Augustine

Guides are not ghosts but beings that are connected by human experience, as we are. They will not impose themselves on us, and if we are afraid they will assure us in a different way. The simplest way is just to speak and tell them your needs, thoughts, feelings, fears and joys, but don't expect them to know everything that is best for you.

Be clear in your intentions though, as you always get what you ask for eventually. It may take a while (no time in spirit) and remember, we are working through our 'stuff', so different energy takes different lengths of time to work through. Try this and see what results you get:

Take a large piece of paper and sit quietly (light a candle and play gentle, healing music). When you are relaxed enough, draw what you feel your Angel/Guide to be; don't worry if you can't draw, you may feel the need to just put colours on the paper or an outline, and that's ok, especially if it's your first attempt. With enough practice, you don't know what you could end up with.

Don't be afraid of this type of communication; remember, this force is working with you and in some ways has to be a part of or connected to you on some level. However, that means taking full responsibility for preparation and intention. In other words, do not dis-respect these forces, as just with everything in life, there is dark as well as light, and prayers of some sort are important. Keep it simple and ask the light to surround you while you make this communication.

> *'Give me beauty in the inward soul; may the outward and the inward man be at one.'* Socrates

Feng Shui:

I decided to include this subject, as I believe it's another important, powerful tool to have a little knowledge of, and as with all the subjects in this book, if it resonates with you, you can take it further.

The general description is wind and water, but it is also known as 'the art of going with the flow', in harmony with heaven and earth (that also includes the self, loved ones and life). I will only touch briefly on this subject, due to the fact that it's very complex and has been studied for centuries.

By the 4th century BC, the Chinese elite consulted shamans and diviners to determine the proper placement of homes, pathways and temples. They sought areas where the elements, especially wind (Feng) and water (Shui), were in harmony. This is why even having a small water feature in the garden will help, as it adds sound and movement and also has a wonderful calming effect.

Feng Shui (pronounced fung sway) may sound grand, but it is simply the art of placement. It means placing things in the 'correct' place, and by correct, I mean the most comfortable place for the item.

Our spirit can express itself through our body, mind and emotions, and our home is where our body resides; just as our spirit resides in our body. Without always being consciously aware of this fact, we are responsive to what is around us and our surroundings will influence our moods. A home for instance would be a different experience if it was near a source of fresh water or protected from harsh winds, and would also affect those who live in it.

So if our spirit is trying to tell us something, one of the ways it can do this is through the energy in the home, as your home or car can offer clues to any imbalance, as these are a representation of your life.

As you read these things, read them simply, almost as if you were a child. What would the windows represent, or the doors, the water system or the drains? All these parts are rather easy to match up.

The windows are your eyes

The doors your entry points

The water system is your emotions.

Feng Shui works by reflecting what's happening in your life. Therefore, your 'essence' is in the home or car and will be affected by thoughts and emotions, and that's how they highlight what is not in balance.

It's okay, I had trouble taking it on at first too, until I found my 'simple' way of thinking about it. If your emotions are out of balance, then the energy you send out will be out of balance too, and since that energy will fill the home or car, it will attract itself to the appliance in question and send it out of balance.

I think that's one of the simplest ways of explaining how the plumbing is letting you know that the emotions in your body are out of sync. Native Americans would simply say the washing machine has a spirit; therefore, it's telling you it's not happy.

Life is forever changing, and if we flow with it, it can be a wonderful journey, but most of us struggle with change of any kind. By recognising and reconnecting with natural elements, we can be revitalised by the currents of life, which can only nourish and enhance our human spirit.

It's all about working out and determining the nature of Chi (energy) at any given time and place. According to Chinese medicine, each season is related to one of the body's five vital organs (they recognise late summer as the fifth season).

Autumn is the time when universal energy moves through our lungs (as each organ produces a state of mind). When the energy of the lungs is unsettled, you could feel grief, loss, nostalgia from past and mourning. Because the weather reflects this, for example leaves dying, we feel worse and the amount of sunlight is less too.

This gets our body to use the reserve of energy that is stored in the liver (look at the word – LIVE-R). Our liver holds our 'animal spirit' and when we feel we can't house our spirit, it leaks.

Put together, the lungs and liver will equal tiredness, gloom, etc. So by not getting things sorted in our life, we store the frustration/anger in our liver chakra. It all makes sense!

The five elements are:

Wood = strong, flexible, growth

Fire = stimulating, transmutes

Earth = supportive

Metal = strong, versatile

Water = cleanses

As I am not trained in the art of Feng Shui I have kept this section brief, but I believe it is an important section. You can learn to 'read' your house and what certain parts represent. For example, if you place a large object in the entrance of your hallway and cannot get past, clearly this is not the most comfortable place for it. This seems to be common sense, but I've added a very basic rule of thumb of what your home represents.

If you buy a book, try to keep it simple, as many books go into this subject in great depth. Also, many are based on the Chinese way of life and the geography could be different, which is why so many people get lost along the way (including myself) and quickly lose interest.

The most helpful tool for me was a video called Sacred Space by Denise Linn, which shows a more simplified version of things, and I would recommend it if you are thinking of clearing your home or your life. Your home is also symbolic of your body:

Ground floor = basic self
First floor = higher self
Attic = mind
Electrics = nervous system
Water = emotions
Toilet = ridding self of past
Bedroom/Bed = where you rest your 'temple'
Fire = your heart centre
Doors = entrances to self
Drawers/Cupboards = where we keep things stored
Ornaments = things you adorn your house with, like our jewellery

Each room speaks for itself. Start by asking yourself how easy it is to enter your house. Does it make people feel welcome, or do you make it difficult for people to get in? Are your door handles faulty in any way (getting a handle on things)?

Your bedroom is a place of rest, but millions of books around will not give your body the message to sleep. Is your bed welcoming or is it difficult for you get to? If that is the case, what is it telling you about the way you respect your rest?

The toilet is very important, as it gets rid of your waste (your past). Because the body has the same messages, you will often find people who have problems with their toilet also have problems with constipation, or the opposite.

What does your house jewellery tell you? Often, ornaments we don't really like are there because they were gifts and we don't want to offend the person who bought them, so we place them in some part of the home. Or they hold a memory of a previous partner and this would create a problem, as it holds the energy of that relationship.

The kitchen and food are a very important part of our lives, but in this day and age it doesn't seem to have the respect it used to have. People are too busy to prepare food and ready meals are a part of our life. This speaks volumes.

If the food we eat is food for the soul, what are you saying to yours? Remember that everything is energy. Do you throw food in the microwave, or prepare it from scratch?

Water, the essence of life and fountains are wonderful stress reducers and make a room look calm. A student could place a fountain in the knowledge area of the room to help with learning. A green-coloured fountain promotes growth and tranquillity, and wind chimes are a lovely way to add tinkling sounds to the room to alter chi.

Because everything is energy, take a little time to look at this situation more closely.

Which one of the following will give off the best energy? Person B, talked about on previous pages, runs to the shops. She has little time, grabs a ready meal, not giving much thought to what she's buying, and doesn't hear the relaxation music being played in the store. She runs into the house, throws it in the microwave and five minutes later it's going on the plate.

Person A, however, goes to the shop and while she's shopping she enjoys the soft relaxation music that's playing. She's enjoying the shopping, and buys fresh food and takes it home to prepare from scratch. Because she's in a good mood, the energy from person A will taste so much better and will obviously be healthier too.

How many of you are reading this and thinking:

'That's okay for her, she's probably not working as much I am,' or,

'I can't afford the luxury of all that.'

I used to think along those lines too and was in victim/martyr mode, so to speak. I couldn't afford fresh good-quality food and so I always bought the cheapest. If something was on special offer I would buy as many as I could and store it. The message to the universe was that I didn't trust it to provide what I needed, as and when I needed it. Usually, a person that stores or hoards has a hang-up from childhood that's saying we must stock up in case we need it one day.

Many people over the past few years have called into the shop to buy a three-legged toad (for good luck), as they know something in their life is not right. However, it's not only a case of buying a little statue to sort out the problem and placing it in the right place to achieve real balance. It's about reading your home like the body.

> *'Genius is a man who has discovered how to increase the intensity of thought to the point where he can freely communicate with sources of knowledge not available through the ordinary state of thought.'* Napoleon Hill, American Author

If all's fine in life then leave everything as it is, but if love or money, etc. aren't coming into your life and you would like them to, you could look at what could be done to change the energy in the areas concerned.

Remember though, if you look at the chakra information you may find why these things are not in your life. Also, when we are in balance we find ourselves happily spring-cleaning and we move things around to where they are suited. This tends to be done when we are feeling enthusiastic (the God within).

By doing the spring-cleaning, we are in fact getting rid of old unwanted or unused items so that fresh new energy can be brought into our life. It's the letting go that's the hardest part, but it is for the best in the long run. But then I'm reminded of a saying an old friend used to have:

'I find something that's good for me, and then don't do it.'

I think that sums it up for a lot of us!

Note on the energy of dream catchers. Dream catchers are good for helping sleep and the traditional dream catchers hold the dreams we want to manifest, while the bad dreams are filtered away by the feathers and transformed (although I have heard it to be the other way round). If a dream catcher is made by an original Native American or someone of like mind, the dream catcher will do the job. Many today are made in factories by people in third world countries on very low pay, so the energy going into the dream catcher could have the opposite effect. I have seen this happen in the past with people having some bad experiences.

CHAPTER 15

TLC

I HAVE CALLED this last chapter TLC because that's what the book is about; Tender Loving Care, for the Self. If you've reached this part of the book, you must have needed to hear the words on some level or you wouldn't be reading them.

Learning to listen to our bodies and to love ourselves is often hard to do due to the life we've had and the programming we have received in life. Understanding that our life is as we have created it is also a very difficult concept to take on, especially if you're having a tough time! But in order to change an unhappy life, this must be integrated into our thinking.

How many people do you know who are working with the 'angel' to try to create love, happiness and joy? How many are working with the 'little devil' that stops us being at peace? Are you creating heaven on earth? Or are you in a living hell? It should be easy to wake up in the morning, breathe deeply, stretch our bodies and look forward to the day ahead with ease, but how many of us do that?

'If you dream it, you can achieve it.' Walt Disney

For many, the day starts with rushing from the bedclothes and popping to the bathroom, on the way to the kitchen to put the kettle on. Swilling a cup of coffee/tea down, and if lucky a slice of toast on the way out the door, and that's for those who don't have to see to another person's needs. It has to stop! We have to give ourselves another form of TLC: TIME, LOVE and CARE.

That means time to smell the roses. By giving ourselves the precious gift of time we can begin to realise that we can achieve anything because we will actually stop for a moment and notice things like flowers, and simply by looking at them actually slows our heart rate down and then we smile.

And remember, smiling releases that honey-like substance from inside.

We should all be able to have time to stretch the body and give it time to wake up properly, to feed it healthily so that it has the fuel to get through a day's work, and the luxury of preparing our self for the day ahead by having quiet time, even if only for ten minutes a day, as ten minutes of breathing deeply with our eyes closed would help us to set our intention for what we want from the day ahead, which would benefit our work too.

But so many people are working too hard at a job they're not happy in to get the things they want in life, like a big house with the latest gadgets, a wardrobe full of designer clothes and a new car, etc. What's the point, when more than three quarters of our life is spent at work, earning money to pay for it all? It doesn't make any sense!

Many years ago, I remember coming home from one of my first jobs at a local well-known store and announcing to my family that I was leaving the job, as I was bored and wanted another one. My uncle was horrified and told me:

'There are no jobs out there; you should feel lucky to have one and stick at it'. But in my heart, I knew that I should follow my heart and so I found another job which fulfilled me more and was also where I met my first husband and learnt so many of life's lessons. So it was a very important move in the end.

What if I hadn't listened to my heart?

Looking back, I know I'd have stayed with my childhood sweetheart and stayed exactly where I was at sixteen. I'd have had a comfortable life with a good man and probably had many children, as he came from a very large Irish family. I'd have been happy, but certainly not fulfilled.

I suppose you may be wondering why I wouldn't wish for this nice alternative life, but you see, without all the joys and hurts from the last thirty-five years I wouldn't have created the twists and turns of my life that have led me to where I am now.

Most importantly, I wouldn't have the children I have, as remember, each child comes with a specific pair of parents, so if I'd stayed with that man, they'd be different children. Therefore, I wouldn't change a thing, because I wouldn't want a life without the children I've been blessed with, and of course now my precious grandchildren. I now realise that without me in the world, they wouldn't exist as they are. That's how important I am in this world! Wow, what a statement

!

'To be nobody but yourself in a world that is doing its best to make you just like everybody else, means to fight the greatest battle there is to fight and to never stop fighting.' E. E. Cummings, American Poet and Painter

Before starting in metaphysics, etc., I couldn't have even thought such a thing, never mind actually believing that I'm that important. Of course, on a 'down day' when my energy runs too low, I don't often say it, and I'll say things to myself that are not very nice.

I may criticise my body or create a little drama, telling myself that I am not loved. In the old days I'd have carried on and turned it into a huge drama, eventually pulling everyone around me into it.

After the chaos had begun and others were drawn in, I'd want it to stop, as I really couldn't see that I'd started it all. I suppose I became that little child who craved attention! After all, if people stay around you when you have caused so much mayhem, then they must love you, mustn't they?

This way of thinking is very third dimensional and very dangerous, as the words we use in our darkest moments can undo any good we have created in our life. The words we speak in such moments can and do create havoc in our lives and the lives of those we love. That's why watching our thoughts is so important, as the 'devil' within can control us just as much as our 'god' can.

I realise these words can be too honest for some people, as it's often said that I'm very honest about my past and how I reached this point in my life. But I believe that is the only way to do it. There's no point in fooling ourselves! But self-delusion is a difficult one to conquer for many, but it's worth it for the end result.

Thankfully, I can now be more aware of my thoughts, and when I do start to go down the self-pity route I reach for a crystal, a tape or a book that 're-minds' me of who I am and what I'm doing, and this will usually lift me back to a place where I want to be.

'When it starts to rain, let it.' Unknown

Although I find I talk to myself a lot more, I can usually sort out the drama in my head before bringing it into my world and affecting those around me. I now call them my down days, and if I am having one, I own it and get through it the best way I can. After all, it's who I am and I now don't believe I can heal the past by covering it up or by constantly raking it up, or even by becoming a different person. After all, the past made me who I am, and thankfully, I'm able to say that I now believe I'm a nice person.

It's taken me a long time, but I've learnt that I can't please everyone, and I stopped trying a while ago, but it comes back to bite me in the bum now and again. What's important is knowing that I love and respect myself, as in knowing that, I take full responsibility for my life and my actions and I know that my intentions are good in all that I do. I cannot ask any more of myself.

Before I finish this section and also the book, I would like to talk a little on the subject of 'going back over', as I put it. Many times while putting this together, I created many hurdles to stop myself from actually finishing it. I couldn't see how or why I'd want to do such a thing, but the part of me (the little devil) that really doesn't believe I can succeed has fought me all the way. Why, you may ask, as I did many times. To fail! It's as simple as that, as we find it easier to fail than to succeed.

For those of you that have started on the journey of self-discovery, please don't give up when you get to a point when you're going one step forward, then ten steps back. I found so many reasons why I shouldn't even bother to finish this project.

I can start things – I've proven that many times – but I seem to have a bit of bother with ending things. When I got to this part of the book I created a bigger drama than I'd had in years, involving my family, friends and career, not to mention money!

Everything that could have brought me problems hit me all at once and I started the self-doubt game. Once again, I doubted whether any of 'this' works and wondered if any of it is real. I never doubted the God-force – *I'm in no doubt that it is there* – but I doubted whether I'd got it right. Had I read the signs wrong?

> '*It isn't the absence of the problem, it is how one lives in the presence, that matters.*' Chungliang Al Huang

Had I worked at it all these years to find a dead end?

At one point, I found myself in a place that I really never thought I'd get out of, and was about to give in. I had been 'forced' (for an unnatural number of reasons) to close down my second business after being told many times from 'upstairs' that it would successfully sell. But that never happened. I asked 'upstairs' what was going on, but didn't receive any answers, which took me to a very dark place within myself and I started doubting everything I believed in.

I swore at 'upstairs' as to why so many things had happened in my life that 'they' could have helped me with. In my darkest hour I blamed 'upstairs' for not telling me that my home was on fire so I could save our cat, or for not telling me when I was being betrayed with my business deal.

I pleaded for answers as to why 'they' allowed me to go ahead with the second business so that it would have to close within two years, and most of all I asked why my world was crumbling around me.

As I've said previously, in those dark pits we can see no light at all. We see only darkness. At these times we can't keep track of our 'shadow side', as our energy is so dark that it blends in and we become one with it!

When you're walking down a street with a light in front of you, your shadow follows you and then, as you get closer, it is by your side and then at some point in front. However, when there is no light shining, we don't get to see our shadow and, metaphorically, this is the same when we're in the pit of despair.

Those times are lonely, as no matter how many people love you, you will only concentrate on those who don't. I spent many weeks crying in that pit. I never answered calls and never went to see my friends. I was so dark that I thought it wasn't right to take my darkness into their world.

I knew in my heart that this was my 'fight' and I had to find ways to get through it that felt right for me. Thankfully, I lived close to the sea and spent many hours thinking as I walked along the shoreline. Then, one morning I finished fighting my situation and 'gave in'. I stopped trying to find the answers, made myself a coffee and sat with my eyes closed for a while.

> 'Only those willing to risk going too far can find out how far they can go.' T. S. Elliot

Then something wonderful happened - I felt a pulling feeling in my brow and saw the colour purple swirling around. Nothing psychic had happened for a while, so I was really excited at this and instead of getting up as I would normally, I sat and let it happen. As the colour expanded I started up a dialogue with 'upstairs' and asked why my life had gone to pot?

My guides started replying in the usual way (with thoughts in my head) and I asked why I don't hear or see them like other mediums do. I was told that each of us is different, so why should my way of working be the same way as other mediums. I let the 'discussion' carry on and then I asked why they had left me when I needed them most. I asked:

'Why don't you stop me from falling into these pits?' and I was told that they cannot stop this, as they are *my* pits.

'Remember, you are creating your reality,' they said. 'Therefore, it is up to you to stop creating the pits, and when you do you can stop falling into them.'

I didn't like the answer (as we often don't), and asked why if they are my *guides* they can't give me a clue before I fall. But again, I was told that I had created them for a reason. The reason, to get me to this moment! Simple as that! Even if it was just so that I would write this section, it would be enough.

But this moment is so much more than that! This moment has so much potential and what I choose to do with it is my responsibility and mine alone. Even if I choose to waste it, that's up to me!

At that moment, I looked back over the nightmare I was in and realised that by creating the huge drama I was once again stopping myself from finishing this book and going into the next phase of my life. Why? Plain and simple – FEAR. The fear was failure and maybe of ending up with nothing. And as I now know we work through the Law of Attraction, it had brought me just that – nothing!

You see, there is no pressure to do anything with our life except to be happy within, yet I hadn't realised that. Plus, if I had moved away I wouldn't be writing this page, I'd probably be doing something very different with my life if I'd lived abroad and I'd have missed all the things I've done in the last few years.

All the wonderful experiences I've had, such as taking my grandchildren to the park and seeing their faces scream with delight as they realise they can climb or slide. I wouldn't have been here to hear my daughter say how important that cuddle was just when she needed it.

> '*The secret of success is making a vocation your vacation.*'
> Mark Twain

It's not right or wrong that I didn't start a new life back then or close/ carry on with my business, because there is no right or wrong way. It's the wondering whether we are doing it right that puts so much pressure on us and it's going back to the programming again. The programming to be a success or to be the best at something, or whatever it is that makes us often flog ourselves to death.

That day I realised I did have a way out of my painful situation; I had my book and by doing what I'd written brought me back to my senses (look at the word) and brought my energy back up! I played high-energy music, lit the incense and lay with my crystals while giving myself Reiki.

I went for long walks, put sea salt in my bath water to clear the negativity, massaged my body and played my hypnotherapy CDs. Surely I hadn't created the last couple of years of chaos just to prove to myself that my theory really does work?

Or had I done just that?

For every drama I've created over the last few years I can see a pattern, the pattern of not being good enough. I originally typed 'God enough' by mistake, but maybe it was a Freudian slip, as God enough is just what was said to me by my daughter a few days before when we were having a discussion on why I recently went into self-destruct mode.

She'd observed that whenever I create something wonderful in my life, like my crystal shop that changed so many lives for the better, I acted as if someone else had created it and that I was just working there.

Whereas if I create disaster, I claim it!

She said she wished I could claim more of the God part of myself.

I knew she was right in saying this (aren't our children wonderful at teaching us things about ourselves) and the more I thought about it the more I knew that, although I talked about God being within, I was actually paying lip service most of the time, especially when it came to loving myself.

> 'Do not wait for leaders: do it alone, person to person.'
> Mother Theresa

I woke the day after that discussion and could hardly move, as my back had 'gone' again and I nearly went into 'here we go again', but I remembered her words, and sat quietly and thought about it all.

I went over recent events in my head and noticed that I'd come to believe that if I changed course altogether it would mean that none of this works. How could I finish a book about self-help when I clearly couldn't help myself? How silly of me! Nothing is ever wasted; everything we do will get us to the moment we are in. This moment is the only thing you have total control over, as remember, the past has already gone and the future hasn't arrived; this moment is a gift, that is why it is called the present.

If I'd followed the signs to close my business and changed direction, and been happy, then it had worked. It doesn't matter what we 'do', it's how we FEEL about what we do that matters. If everything's going well and life's a peach, then you are exactly where you are meant to be, in a place of healthy love.

But when things are tough, or you can't seem to get it right and the world looks as if it's against you, it's only your higher self (YOU) trying to get a message to YOU that it may not be travelling down the best road. You then have the choice to either carry on or change direction. But it's YOUR choice.

Personal responsibility is a hard fact of life, and I don't think enough people in the world use it. But then I think that is because of the world we have created; it's become easier to blame another force, be it a person (such as a boss, partner, child, friend or parent) or an outside force such as our past, our class, etc., or that outside force called GOD.

The fight with myself to keep the shop open, stay in my hometown or even go away and start a new life was just that, my fight.

The fight stops when we reach a point when we are true to ourselves and that's all we can hope to be, as to be a success in anything is of no use if your heart is not happy. It's no use saying:

'I'll be happier when I get more money,' or

'I'll do more when the children leave home,' as these and so many other excuses are just that. Let's face it, we might not have tomorrow, it's certainly not guaranteed, we only have this moment.

'Dream as if you'll live forever. Live as if you'll die tomorrow.'
James Dean

I hope that you've enjoyed reading this book and that I have at least opened a door for you into the world of energy, metaphysics, etc., and that I've made it an easy and enjoyable journey. My intention of this book is not to heal anyone, it's to open a doorway to a new way of looking at your life and your body, and allow it to awaken to the ability of contributing to 'healing' your life.

I really do believe that if this information is taken on, then understanding our lives and its purpose will make the journey of life a more enjoyable one.

Understanding why hurt comes into our lives can only make us stronger, and once that's taken onboard we are rarely the 'victim' again. We learn to take responsibility for our thoughts and actions, and when something goes 'wrong' in our lives we'll be able to turn it around more easily.

So many people think that sending out a harmful thought or screaming abuse at someone won't affect the other person, but it does, it affects all of us. The energy we transmit from our system is so important, especially now, as we are going into a very important stage in evolution.

We have the chance to make a difference to the world, simply by changing ourselves, and by bringing more peace, honesty and harmony into our life we can then help to support those around us.

We are simply a projector (third eye) sending our thoughts on to the screen of life. We are the writers (generators), directors (organisers) and producers (deliverers) of our life, or we can simply hand it all over to others to produce; it's up to us.

The following quiz is useful in seeing how balanced your energy system is, but make sure you answer each question honestly:

Score one point for column one, two points for column two, three points for column three and four points for column four. Add up the points for each chakra before moving to the next one.

Answer all questions with one of the following:
Never/Seldom/Often/Always
Poor/Fair/Good/Excellent

Chakra One: Earth, Survival, Grounding

How often do you go for a walk in nature?
How often do you exercise?
How is your financial situation?
How would you rate your diet?
Do you consider yourself well grounded?
Do you feel supported by your family in having what you want out of life?

Chakra Two: Emotions, Sexuality

How would you rate your ability to express your emotions?
How would you rate your sex life?
How often do you show nurturing for others?

Do you allow yourself to relax and seek pleasure?
How would you rate your physical flexibility?
How would you rate your emotional flexibility?

Chakra Three: Fire, Power

How would you rate your sense of personal power?
How would you rate the effectiveness of your will?
How would you rate your daily energy level?
How would you rate your metabolism?
Do you accomplish what you set out to do?
Do you feel confident?

Chakra Four: Air, Love

How often do you feel happy?
How would you rate your ability to make friends?
Do you love yourself?
Do you feel connected to the world around you?
Do you have successful long-term relationships?
Do you feel in harmony with your present situation?

Chakra Five: Sound, Communication

How would you rate your ability to communicate your ideas?
Do you listen well to others' ideas?
Are you creative?
How would you rate the resonance of your voice?
Do you harmonise well with others?
Do you engage in an art form, painting, music, dance, writing, etc.?

Chakra Six: Light, Clairvoyance

Do you notice visual details in your surroundings?
Do you have vivid dreams?
Do you have psychic experiences, i.e. precognitions, uncanny coincidences?
How do you rate your ability to visualise?
Do you make use of your imagination?
Do you like bright colours?

Chakra Seven: Thought, Understanding

Do you meditate?
Do you have strong spiritual experiences?
Do you spend a lot of time intellectualising?

Do you spend time gathering information, researching, studying, etc.?
Are you consciously aware of your thoughts, actions, motives, etc.?
Do you have faith in your own intuition/inner voice?

A score of 21–24 indicates a very strong chakra, 6–12 indicates a weaker chakra. However, it is the distribution that is important. Compare your scores between different parts. Aside from the strongest and weakest chakras, is there a distribution pattern, e.g. higher scores in lower chakras, or higher scores in upper or middle chakras? Does this pattern coincide with your own views and how you perceive yourself?

If you had an unwanted guest, would you keep feeding the guest knowing this would make them stay longer? Illness is the same. So if your energy is low, look at how to raise it and try to do this before it becomes so low that you will need another person to help get yourself back on track. Depending on the issue that is lowering your energy, you can try these few suggestions:

✻ Sit and do diaphragm breathing (in through nose, letting belly fill out and breathe out through the mouth, letting belly in).

✻ Take a shower and picture water as white light coming into your crown and the negativity being washed down the plughole, or have a bath with sea salt in it.

✻ Sit for a few minutes with a crystal and literally have a word with yourself, asking what the real problem is.

✻ Go for a walk in nature.

✻ Play a Guided Meditation CD.

✻ Exercise.

These and many more are ways to lift your energy and keep you 'high'. The body is a great reflection of what is happening to you at any particular time, so ask what it's trying to tell you. Whatever you choose, just enjoy it and most of all, be happy. It's not a crime, it is our birthright. I was sent this next fable by my friend Linda and decided to include it in a talk I was facilitating at a Mind, Body and Spirit day, and I will share it with you:

THE MOUSE STORY

A mouse looked through the crack in the wall to see the farmer and his wife open a package. 'What food might this contain?' the mouse wondered. He was devastated to discover it was a mousetrap. Retreating to the farmyard, the mouse proclaimed the warning,

'There is a mousetrap in the house! There is a mousetrap in the house!'

The chicken clucked and scratched, raised her head and said,

'Mr Mouse, I can tell this is a grave concern to you, but it is of no consequence to me.

I cannot be bothered by it.'

The mouse turned to the pig and told him,

'There is a mousetrap in the house! There is a mousetrap in the house!'

The pig sympathised, but said,

'I am so very sorry, Mr Mouse, but there is nothing I can do about it but pray. Be assured, you are in my prayers.'

The mouse turned to the cow and said,

'There is a mousetrap in the house! There is a mousetrap in the house!'

The cow said,

'Wow, Mr Mouse. I'm sorry for you, but it's no skin off my nose.'

So the mouse returned to the house, head down and dejected, to face the farmer's mousetrap all alone.

That very night a sound was heard throughout the house, like a mousetrap catching its prey. The farmer's wife rushed to see what had been caught. In the darkness, she did not see that it was a venomous snake whose tail the trap had caught. The snake bit the farmer's wife! The farmer rushed her to the hospital and she returned home with a fever. Everyone knows you treat a fever with fresh chicken soup, so the farmer took his hatchet to the farmyard to get the soup's main ingredient.

His wife's sickness continued; friends and neighbours sat with her around the clock. To feed them, the farmer butchered the pig. The farmer's wife did not get well and she died.

So many people came to her funeral that the farmer had the cow slaughtered to provide enough meat for them all. The mouse looked upon it all from his crack in the wall with great sadness!

So, the next time you hear someone is facing a problem and think it doesn't concern you, remember … when one of us is threatened, we are all at risk. We are all involved in this journey called life and we must keep an eye out for one another and make an extra effort to encourage others. Each of us is a vital thread in another person's tapestry, as every thought we have affects the planet and our lives are woven together for a reason.

> '*If you want to be happy for an hour – take a nap.*
> *If you want to be happy for a day – go fishing.*
> *If you want to be happy for a month – get married.*
> *If you want to be happy for a year – inherit a fortune.*
> *If you want to be happy for a lifetime – help others.*'
>
> Old Chinese Proverb

Yes, a few years ago I DID have everything, but in my heart something was missing and although I'd worked very hard for the life I had I knew I had to be true to myself; therefore, I had to do something about it.

I asked the Source to support me, and even though it has been very tough at times, I really do believe it did and still is. That frightened little 'Border Girl' actually did what she had only dared to dream of doing.

To stand on the Blue Lagoon on Morton Island in Australia at midnight and watch a shower of shooting stars and to camp on the very site where Aborigines slept are things she could never have dreamt to be possible, but she did it! How? Because I learnt to believe in the system called God and, most of all, to believe in myself.

Through all the turmoil of letting go of the house and then the shops, I found freedom for the first time in my life and I've certainly learnt a lot about people along the way. I've learnt that my health is of utmost importance, and that the love for my family and my true friends will always be, because love is the only thing that is real.

I've learnt to read the signs of the universe, which isn't always easy, but so worthwhile when we do. I used to think of heaven as being a place where God sits, and believed that if I am good I'll get to go there and be in ecstasy. But I now know that these are states of mind (of being). The higher we vibrate, the nearer and clearer we can see (clairvoyance) and will be able to connect with that higher force (our higher self that has OUR answers) that can help us achieve our true potential.

Yet, the ego (lower mind) doesn't want that and we begin what I have come to call the superman battle (in the film he fights with himself in the scrap yard). The lower mind wants us to stay in what it is familiar, with chaos, and a sort of better-the-devil-you-know attitude.

I have asked myself many times why the lower mind would want to do this, and certain books I've read over the years do offer explanations, but although they make sense at the time of reading, living them isn't as easy and I often slipped back into the chaos.

It's obviously what I'm familiar with and a recent conversation with my daughter proved it. She always says she wishes I could stop creating the chaos and pain and refers to my 'onion', which is finally peeling away (the onion referring to the layers of issues we have; layers of belief about our self and our world). She also stated that some people working through their issues have only had a couple of major events in their life, *not hundreds*, as I have.

That's true I suppose, as when I finished one illness or dis-ease thinking, *Thank God that's over*, I'd find another drama of some sort following closely behind. What's happening now, I'd ask? What's been the point of getting into all this spiritual life, if my life is still in constant chaos?

Well, I suppose the difference now is that I don't believe that God doesn't like me or that I'm being punished for being a 'bad girl'. Now I believe the chaos is something I'm working on to achieve that higher level of being. Mind you, on a 'down day' I still ask why I bother. But I just know it will all be worth it once I've worked through all my 'stuff', as I'll finally live in joy more and more.

The roller coaster of life will always have its ups and downs, the difference is that now I have an awareness of how I can deal with these and turn them around instead of staying down and waiting for someone else to make it better for me. I believe living in this state will bring in whatever my heart truly desires. I'll be an alchemist, who can turn lead into gold.

Many people believe tales of alchemists are just fantasy, but if we change the word 'wizard' in these tales to 'guide', we can get a clearer picture of how we can talk to that part of us that has the answers. That knowledge we just can't grasp, we own; our intuition, as we are both the questioner and the wizard with the answers and we hear its voice in the silence called meditation.

As our self-image is built upon all our past memories and programmes, creating the 'I', the type of 'I' we own is due to what beliefs we've heard around us. We can all be brave one day and a coward the next, and whichever part of us is in control at the time is the one that will dominate the day.

Our wizard/guide is beyond all opposites such as good/evil, light/

dark, pleasure/ pain, and it's the duality we've created that causes so much pain in our world, as we feel disconnected and often wander through life 'alone'. It's the ego part of ourselves that lets us believe we are alone, which of course we can never be, as we are all one and all part of the whole energy system called life.

But because we feel separate from the source of life (the wizard or guide within), we feel alone and therefore we create fear, and maybe this fear creates the ego so we don't feel alone and the circle continues. When you know your guide, you will realise that the outer world merely reflects the moods and desires of the inner world. In our other levels of consciousness, we have the ability to create whatever we want. Therefore, it's in the silence that we create and I now realise why meditating is so important.

Our wise inner being knows the secrets of immortality: that we never die and there was therefore never a time when we didn't exist in some form or another. If you can't get to grips with this concept, just think of gold. Gold can be a ring, necklace or an ornament, but it's still gold; it doesn't matter what form it takes. The same can be said of certain foods and it's the same with us; we are always spirit, just taking on another form.

Meditation is about getting in contact with our core self, beyond the inner dialogue where our silence is, and doing it even in a small way will benefit us. I suppose the solitude we are seeking in meditation is like a pit stop for the soul; daily spells of looking within for answers that can help us find how to live a healthy, happy life, as the solitude connects us to our creative source and releases the limitless intelligence of the universe.

Purification is the moving out of old limitations that grip us and the old beliefs that play over and over and need clearing, as they no longer serve us. Therapies are helpful in this area, but so are simple things like walking in nature. Honesty and self-awareness are important issues too, and remember, don't squash feelings down, let them go.

Awareness and attention are about noticing reality when it peeks out from illusion, such as synchronicity, or using things like angel cards and the like, which are ways that our spirit can get a message to us. Look for events that allow your spirit to show you that it's trying to draw your attention to something. Ask for signs and act on them, and simply practising these three things will get your life to change.

Having a spare room or part of a room that's just for your silence (your sacred space) will make all the difference, and try to meditate at the same time each day, as it's more effective since it becomes part of a ritual.

Stillness is the stepping stone to connecting with the universal source; that intelligence that throbs through every living thing. As said to me on a recent local radio interview, 'If you don't go within, you go without.'

Every memory and wish that has been collected creates all the personalities that make us who we are. Therefore, it has to start with peace within the self, as if we don't make peace with ourselves we will be like a time bomb and explode or even implode, creating a dis-ease or illness.

As I reach the end of this book, I'm back where I started in my hometown after again following the signs; I can't wait to see what my next step will be – that's when I decide what I want it to be. It's taken me a while to understand why I had to give up everything I had, but I followed my heart and experienced complete freedom on many occasions, and that's been priceless.

I realise now that I had to stop fighting myself and stand up for myself more, but most importantly, I had to be true to myself and ask my heart what it really wanted in life. I really do believe that the body talks to us, and that if the information of the body language plus the chakra/auric system is learnt and followed, then following our heart and understanding our purpose will make the journey of life a more enjoyable one.

Understanding why hurt comes into our lives can only make us stronger and we must learn to take responsibility for our decisions. Although sometimes it can be too difficult to look closely at what we FEEL is wrong in life, it must be done.

Some choices are just too difficult to make, and for those who choose not to follow their heart that's okay too, because each action we take is ours to make and therefore our response-ability. That simply means having the ability to respond, or not, to a thought or feeling.

I don't regret giving everything up to go travelling, as I thoroughly enjoyed each experience, although sometimes, in my dark moments of fear, I think I may have come full circle in some issues; a little like the boy in *The Alchemist* by Paulo Coelho. As the book says: '*The only thing that stops us from fulfilling our dreams is the fear of failure.*'

I realised in the end that I have to stop using other people to fill me up. I need to create my own happiness by detaching from my dependencies on others, as if peace in my heart is dependent on how others are going to act then I'm living in the realm of the lower self and will always be in constant conflict.

Now, when I'm feeling down, I ask:

'What would my higher self say about all this?'

When I have to make a decision, I try asking as an observer and say:

'I wonder what Marie would do,' and then I try to distance myself from the drama. If it's a particularly tough drama, I say:

'Okay, universe, take over please. Whatever happens, so be it.'

I've learnt to trust the grand design more. Then I turn it over and get on with the day, stopping now and again to listen to my intuitive mind. I even began setting my phone alarm at certain intervals to remind myself to sit quietly and see if I had given myself enough attention.

When we focus on abundance, our life feels more abundant. When we focus on lack, our life feels like it is lacking something. It's simply a matter of focus. It's not setting the goal that's the problem, it's the hanging on to the outcome of it, and our lower self has fun with this as it's always reminding us that it won't work out.

When I began this way of thinking, I didn't give myself a hard time if things went wrong, as I knew I was a beginner and didn't have all the answers. Yet, during this last crisis I did give myself a hard time, as I thought I should have known all the answers. But it's not that simple, is it? I now realise there is something within me that has a bigger plan for my life than I'm capable of imagining and when I fully engage in the dialogue, I will fully understand where I am heading.

We need to take ourselves out of the comfort zone to explore the unknown and do what we dare to dream, but too often, we fool ourselves into thinking we can't. By being the person we dream to be, we live the life we were meant to have, as fear is only conditioned response and habit.

When we erase fear from our mind, we can look and feel younger and are healthier. We owe it to ourselves to do what makes us happy, because if we can't manage that, how can we manage anything else?

Happiness isn't something unachievable, it comes through good judgment, good judgment comes through experience and experience often comes through bad judgment. It's only when we repeat the same mistakes over and over without learning from them that we show a lack of self-awareness. Our mind is nature's greatest gift to us and yet we use only 1/100th of a per cent, and as we know all too well with the mind, it's a case of use it or lose it. The way we think is from pure and simple habit and the secret of life management is simply mind management. But we've been trained to worry and yet worry actually drains us of our energy; it's like trying to continue on a bike journey with the inner tube deflated. The journey will end, unless we inflate the tube with air (energy) to continue.

Fatigue is a huge problem at the moment for many people, but it's often a creation of the mind. It dominates the lives of those with no purpose or goals; after all, if someone came along and suggested doing something you really wanted to do, then the tiredness would leave immediately. This shows that when we often say we can't do something because we are too tired, it's more often than not the fact that we don't really want to do it.

Reading the signs in life makes the learning easier. Indigenous people would even 'read' the animals and insects that were nearby and it's fascinating to learn how each one would give them a message.

Unfortunately, we don't come across many wild animals in our daily lives and now we have to rely on the cards created by people such as Jamie Sands and his *Animal Cards*, to give us the messages of the animal kingdom. Here are a few animals/insects with a brief message you might come across in daily life:

Ant – be patient
Butterfly – transformation
Deer – be gentle with yourself
Dragonfly – confront denials
Eagle – connect with spirit
Frog – tears, cleansing
Horse – honour your medicine
Hawk – see the bigger picture
Spider – dance your dreams alive, create from your heart
Squirrel – gather the rewards of stewardship

You can make your own meanings too, as with a message from my mother after we'd had the fire. A medium at church said that when I saw a robin, it was my mam telling me everything would start to change and get better. As it was May at the time, I wasn't too impressed that I would have to wait till Christmas for things to improve.

However, I didn't have to wait long, as on a visit to the country in June, I saw a robin sat on a log in bright sunshine and I knew that was my sign. Ever since, I've seen robins in the most unusual places and at the strangest times. This has become my mam's sign that she's near and that things are going to be all right.

For those who are cynical as to whether things would have got better anyway or who think that because I saw it I changed my thoughts, it doesn't really matter. In *my world*, a robin now means my mother is near and that's all that matters.

Another way to create your dreams is to make a dream book/box or dream board that you fill with pictures and descriptions of what you desire. You can have sections for relationships, career, holidays, fitness and financial goals. If want a cottage by the sea, fill that section with pictures and items that will bring it to life.

By looking at it often, you are giving it energy and focus, and therefore, you'll bring it into your life. How quickly you do will depend on how much energy you give it, and of course how much you really FEEL you deserve it. But remember that your intention is of the utmost importance; if you're asking out of greed, the outcome may not be as healthy as planned. Happy dreaming!

As well as giving thanks for my children in this book, I must dedicate and thank my children for their love and support, although at times they may have thought me a little wacko since I started on this journey.

I also dedicate this book to my friends (even the ones I am no longer in contact with) who have supported me throughout some of the most painful situations in the last 25 years. Without them, I certainly wouldn't be the person I am now. In the past they've been there whenever I've needed them, especially taking care of my children while I worked or became ill and had to be hospitalised (too many times before I learnt about this way of thinking). Although at times they might not have understood me, they gave me the love, support and, most importantly, the laughter that I needed.

I believe that realising how important our thoughts are is one of the most significant things I've learnt on my journey of self-discovery. It's an ongoing thing to watch out for, as it's very easy to slip into old thinking patterns.

We should, or a more empowering word is *could*, be watching what energy leaves our system and be totally responsible for bringing harmony to this beautiful world of ours.

This planet is indeed very beautiful and it's our responsibility to make sure we have a planet to pass down to other generations. If we take more care of our thoughts and our energy in general, we will hand down a healthier world. Wouldn't that be nice?

I hope many of you take these subjects further, as they are very empowering, but whatever you do, be aware of which energy you are working with. Most importantly, enjoy the journey and, as I leave you, I wish you all that I wish myself.

Epilogue

SINCE FINISHING this book I had an 'accident' that led to me being hospitalised due to a fall that fractured a bone in my already damaged spine. As I lay there waiting for the ambulance to arrive, I really thought my walking days were over, as I'd landed with such force on the ground.

Once again, all my fears came back to haunt me. I'd dreaded being ill in any way, as I knew what would be thrown at me about my beliefs. Previously, if I'd had a cold or backache it would be said, 'Well, your healing doesn't seem to work, does it?'

I was in hospital for four days, in which time they found I had osteoporosis and arthritis too, and my many demons came to stay with me in that time, taunting me that all I believe in was false. Once again, I asked the question, 'What's going on?' as I really felt I'd let myself down.

Once I was allowed home, I fought for weeks with depression, isolation, much pain and frustration about the whole situation. I went through the whole denial stage, once again falling into not believing that I could have created it. At one point I thought I was 'hexed' as I'd had so many unfortunate things happen to me in the previous two years, including the certain extremist people actually threatening me and wishing me harm.

> '*Imagination is more important than knowledge.*'
>
> Albert Einstein

However, when my energy lifted a little I started with my healing CDs and looking back over my books and charts to see if I could body map what had happened. I looked at each problem in depth and read what the meanings were, and once again I was amazed at the accuracy of it all.

Once I thought I'd '*cracked it*' (look at my language), I realised a pattern was there and, yet again, it pinpointed a certain childhood programming belief that I was still holding on to. As I had nothing to do but lay around, I started to read the journals I'd written while travelling and made notes on my entries that often referred to being lonely, no one caring or not belonging anywhere. I certainly didn't like some of the 'poor me' referrals I'd made, and once again, down the spiral I went.

Eventually, after reaching the bottom of the pit that I'd become so acquainted with in my life, I cried out to God and my guides for some answers to it all. That same evening, in the early hours, I was woken to hear the words:

'It began in November 1955.'

I tried to move my body, but I was in so much pain even after three weeks of rest and tried to go back to sleep, but I heard it again. I opened my eyes and said aloud:

'Yes, I was born then,' but then I realised that November wasn't the month of my birth. Still shuffling to get comfortable, I wondered what the message meant and then I saw a picture in my mind of a pillow being put over the face of a baby.

I knew the baby was me, as I'd always known that my mam had come to the end of her tether one day when she couldn't cope; I thought I'd just accepted it, but the pain of it was obviously much deeper than I'd thought.

Thoughts started coming in thick and fast, in all directions, and one of them was from a reading I had been given by a Native American lady when I had been in New Mexico the year before. In the reading she told me of the big changes occurring in my life, but that there was a childhood memory that still had a big negative effect on me and was haunting my life (at the time I just thought she was referring to my abuse). I was then reminded of the body mapping I'd been doing over the previous few days.

I was literally being shown how my life had been crumbling away in the previous two years (since November 2005), exactly fifty years from the date given. No! Could this really be the clue I had been trying to find? Had this painful memory been stored on a cellular level all this time?

I turned a few times, trying to make sense of it all, and then the heat started (that's the feeling when I know my guide is with me) and I *felt* I had been given the missing piece of the jigsaw. The time before my *awakening*, I'd been dogged with the thoughts of 'No one cares for me,' etc., and these thoughts battered my brain constantly while lying there alone.

The accident had left my body weak and I was trying to cope without asking for help. I didn't want to ask, and I wanted others to ask me what I needed. Normally, my family and friends would be there taking care of my needs, but for some strange reason they weren't, and for ten days I was very hurt and confused. Once again, I wondered why I had put myself in this awful situation.

That morning at 4 am I had to make sense of what was happening, and so I found a pen and started writing again. I realised that over the previous fourteen months, the life that I knew had started to crumble. I remembered that back then in November 2005 my first physical problem had occurred in the base chakra area, which is linked to my roots/core.

This situation continued and then a further extremely painful experience rocked my entire foundation; at one point, I lost almost everything I loved. At the time my business was affected by the events and it, too, was crumbling under me. Instead of moving forward, I continued trying to hold my old life together and this drained me physically, emotionally and mentally. What I didn't know at the time was that my body was reflecting this too. In reality, I was clinging to a life I was no longer really part of.

I knew that my back had played up on many occasions, but I didn't read the signs properly, dismissed them and carried on. I was fighting the changes all the way. I didn't want to be the lady in the tarot readings I'd had with an important job to do. I wanted to be the mother who's there for her children and the nana who bakes cakes. I also still wanted to be the party girl going out with my friends, but this was proving to be so difficult to achieve, as everything seemed to go against it.

My body was certainly a reflection of the fight I was going through and the weeks preceding what I was *re-minded* of (the word remind means to bring back memories into our consciousness) had been so painful, but I learnt a lot and I walked in a few people's shoes too.

I certainly learnt how hard it must be for the old and infirm just waiting for someone to call in and ask if they need anything, or even just waiting for someone to talk to. This had never happened to me in *my adult life*, but that morning I was reminded that in my childhood, that loneliness was something I'd lived with daily.

I don't mean that I didn't feel love as a child, I somehow *knew* my mother loved me, but I wasn't cared for the way a child should be. The events after the accident had reminded me of the fact that I had been a child that was never wanted, and this belief had been embedded into my very being.

For those who are still having a hard time understanding how or why we would bring in illness and disease, I've included a section from the Martin Brofman book, which explains it from the biological perspective, but I still highly recommend that you get a copy and read this fascinating story of a very special man:

'*Physical sciences are based on ideas that the cause of a symptom is outside us (i.e. germs, accidents, etc.) but in Metaphysics these events can only happen if proper conditions are in our consciousness, sort of like a parallel. Consciousness isn't only in the brain but in the entire body, i.e. through consciousness you are in contact with every part of the body, in and around it (aura), so from the biological point of view, the smallest bio unit being the cell, which is composed of atoms (or ions). These are composed of particles (neutrons, protons, electrons) that are composed of smaller particles (quarks, neutrons, gluons etc.), which are in turn composed of tiny black holes and white holes, each with a positive charge or a negative one.*

Patterns of these holes, energy, form the smallest of what we call particles and patterns of these form atoms. Patterns of atoms form molecules and they form cells, cells form tissue and tissue forms organs. Patterns of organs form organisms. Therefore, all symptoms are reflections of blocked energy, and by unblocking it by making different decisions or by healing, the symptom is released. Tension in part of a body reflects one aspect of life. When we don't listen to our inner voice, we experience tension and unhappiness. The experience happens so we can reach the end result, therefore attracting attention to it. It only takes an instant to make the decision to heal, the hardest part seems to be to hold on to the perception that it is happening'.

I knew I was being shown something very special that morning, as I was also shown a memory of when I was weeding the garden in our family home. I was with my eldest grandson and I was showing him how to pull the dandelion roots from the ground. As anyone with these flowers in the garden knows, if you do not get the WHOLE root out, it simply grows back again.

My guide had shown me the same image a few years previously too, but I obviously chose to forget this important message, so here it was being shown again. I thought I'd addressed my insecurities about my childhood, but it was perfectly clear I had not. I knew I had to look closely at this again and *work out* (working it out literally means working it out of your field) what was going on inside me!

I was in fact holding on to a life that really wasn't working for me and every corner I turned seemed to be wrong for me. Yet, I know that holding on to something too tight will just suffocate and make it stagnate and that's unhealthy for everyone. But that's what I'd been doing with the people I loved.

I was being given a chance to do what I'd wanted to do for a while, be free, but if I was honest, I was scared they would forget me if I went away. What an unhealthy way to think. There's a saying that to be healthy in the mind is to be healthy in the body, and my mind was in a very unhealthy state, which was reflecting in my body.

Whatever part of our body is out of whack will show by what is happening in our life. If we ignore our intuition, we will end up with some sort of tension, which will eventually lead to unhappiness. This is our body's way of attracting attention to the area that needs looking at, so that the root of it can be back-tracked to the first showing of the tension, and then the issue is released and the stuck energy is freed. The area will then return to free-flowing energy, bringing harmony to the situation and the body.

When there is tension in our thoughts or beliefs we will experience it in the chakra, which will affect the endocrine gland, which will secrete hormones, changing the chemistry in the body part. As we direct energy with thought (remember, where thought goes, energy flows), we, too, have the power to unblock whatever created the tension in the first place.

Alas, when we don't accept a part of who we are, what we did or what we are doing, there can be a reversal in our energy system and the outcome is an unconscious act of sabotage against our goals and desires. Like most things in life, I learnt this the hard way, as I had a difficult time making peace with some of the unhealthy choices that I've made in my life.

But again, if I had made different ones the outcome would be different, and therefore I do not know if that would have made a better outcome than the one I have. I realise that we can only do what we feel is right at the time we are faced with a situation. That is all we can ask of ourselves, as we certainly cannot go back and change our actions, although that little devil on my shoulders tries often enough.

There is no right or wrong here, just cause and effect.

No guilt, just acknowledging responsibility and being total honest with the self. Whichever way of 'being' creates a symptom; we have the decision of which way it then goes. Once we have the knowledge that anything can be healed, we can even heal a situation before it hits the physical layer.

We will not need to receive messages through illness and drama if we take guidance from our inner voice and follow it. It's said that's how the indigenous people lived and how it will be after 2012, but many people are putting this into practice now and finding harmony. For me, I'm still working on it, but now I work with awareness.

Illness and accidents come into our lives for various reasons. They can be to draw our attention to something not right in our life, to alert us of a change of direction that's needed or to something very deep in our consciousness that we would like to clear out of our system.

I see the body as the vehicle to be able to learn to walk, talk, feel, etc. and as with any child that learns to walk, it does so by falling over many times. We are the same! We stumble and stagger, losing control sometimes, but as long as we can get back up and carry on, we're still in the game.

I now view that the lower chakras are like a child being guided by the higher self (higher chakras), there to guide us when we're a little lost or tired of trying. Maybe the 'inner child' that's talked about isn't only referring to our childhood memories. Maybe it's the child part of our soul that resides within.

Could that be why only Yogis, etc. would use the kundalini energy and raise it to see insights? Is it because we are here to master the energy in the lower three chakras in our lifetime? With evolution changing maybe the rest of the chakras are coming into play and for some people even using the ones beyond the physical body, the higher chakras.

Imagine the higher self as having the reins, holding on and guiding the lower self in this life, some with long reins and some not so long. Some even have extending ones, which get tangled up and the guardian has to free the child. I suppose most of us are so eager to experience life that we refuse to stay close enough to receive any help, as we think we know best. Yet, if we looked to our guardians now and again we could have an easier journey, as we wouldn't need to use up as much energy untangling ourselves.

'*Man's mind stretched to a new idea never goes back to its original dimension.*' Oliver Wendell Holmes, American Poet, Writer and Physician

I watched a programme a while ago where hypnotist Derren Brown had a selection of people locked in a room. He told them that if they could get the pointer to reach 100, they would each receive some money. They didn't know how the pointer would change and they started doing things that they thought would make the numbers go higher.

Most of them wanting to achieve the goal scattered about the room, believing that their actions were making it happen. They had no idea that in the next room, each time a goldfish passed a line, the pointer was going up. They hadn't a clue that the outcome had nothing to do with them.

The other thing Derren had done was put a sign on the ceiling, which told them they could walk out at any time as the door was no longer locked and also that if they did this the reward would be bigger. But no one looked up. They were too busy trying to change the outcome and complete the task.

As I watched, I kept thinking that's how we are in the world, running around like headless chickens, trying to reach the goal and the reward. Yet, if we took time to 'look up' now and again, we would see what's really happening and receive a bigger reward. If we slowed down and stepped out for a while, we'd realise that there's a bigger picture going on and that we're not the only ones running the show.

For those that do the journey, it's great. For those who decide not to finish it, that's okay too. The choice is ours and what we do will depend on the kind of situation we find ourselves in, as some situations we find ourselves in literally take away our judgment, therefore making it practically impossible for us to get out of it. After all, some illnesses, accidents and diseases could come in and change our lives simply because we need the experience. Unfortunately, only our soul will know the true reason.

> *'Many people's destiny is a continuous repetition of their history.'*
> James Arthur Ray

I came to realise that I'd been fighting the label of 'disability', which was looping me further into it. I realised that when I was working in my shops, I seemed to have more energy and certainly more enthusiasm, which made me feel more alive. I suppose I was just happier, as I was doing something I loved.

I have now made peace with my 'ailments' and will carry on trying to heal them completely; after all, certain animals can re-grow tails, etc. so maybe we will when we truly believe we can.

I accept now that I have a disability, but do not accept that I am 'dis-abled' (energy of each word is very different). When I did the body mapping, all of my injuries had revealed that I was in fear of moving forward in life (left foot), that I had a core belief that I wasn't cared for (skeleton) and that my inner child and self-confidence were broken (where the injury in my spine was). It also showed the fear from my oldest programming – that I wasn't wanted by those I loved or that I was a pest to everyone around me.

My GOD (generator-organiser-deliverer) was using all my energy to focus on the word/subject, and because the projector of the 'movie' throws out what is on the reel (focus), that is what will be shown (lived) on the screen (our world/life).

At the time, when more and more physical disease came in, the further down the road I went and, at one time, I was advised to claim disability allowance to help my income, as I couldn't work. In my heart I knew that if I accepted it, it would keep me in the role of a disabled person. The words disability and disabled sounded loud and clear!

Maybe I wasn't 'able' to do as many things as I once could, but I still had a lot of me that worked perfectly and I started to focus on them instead. I picked up my books once again and set off on another journey to self-healing, which meant I had to finally transform any negative feelings into positive ones.

This meant turning it around by being grateful for what I could do instead of moaning about what I couldn't do. I started to be thankful that I didn't have anyone relying on me when I was ill, instead of moaning that I didn't have anyone around me. See the difference in this way of thinking?

Most importantly, I started to be aware of my feelings in each situation and to be honest with myself and those around me. I started to rekindle the love feeling that I'd experienced years before when I first opened my shop. At the time, I tried to explain it as being in love, but I didn't have a partner so this confused me.

Up until that point, I didn't realise that love didn't have to come from another and that it was inside all along. I began to realise that the wonderful feeling of warmth that swept over and through me was the wonderful feeling of self-love. It had been inside me all along, but I didn't know that I could access it at anytime by simply being true to my needs, feelings and truths.

I learnt to state my desires, to share my feelings and to speak my truths to the world, but this took a while, as I kept arguing with myself. But my body kept reflecting what I was feeling about situations and eventually, I got tired of being unwell and began to do what I had been advised to do by so many (including 'upstairs') – I started sitting each day and setting my intentions of what I desired. I didn't realise I was meditating!

Eventually, I began to realise that if I listened to my feelings, I wouldn't have to get the message through pain and illness. Eureka moment! My son laughed when I told him, as he said I'd known it for years and taught it to him, yet I always chose the hard way.

Back again to the programming of 'if something's worth having, you must work hard for it'. I now realise that spiritual growth is slow and there are no quick fixes. Spiritual growth is never-ending; it's not a destination, it's to live, and there is always more to learn. Mostly, I learnt that when we think nothing is happening, it is, as an unseen world of energy is moving and changing all the time, in and around us.

My very first programming was being told that I was loved, but I wasn't shown it (due to violence, which gives a child mixed messages of what love really is) and I knew it had dogged my life for long enough. Once again, it was time to let go...

This time, I was letting go of something so much bigger than a business, a car etc. I was finally letting go of my oldest belief that I'd held on to for far too long, the patterns that had sabotaged most of my relationships.

This had indeed been a very painful time for me, but one that at least I knew was going to be a very healthy one in the long run, as I prepared to go through the final stages of my healing and into the second part of my life.

I wonder what I shall create next?

> '*Seek ye first the kingdom of heaven within, and then all else will be given unto you.*' Jesus of Nazareth

RECOMMENDED BOOKS

Broffman, Martin	*Anything Can Be Healed* (2003) Findhorn Press Ltd.
Brown, Dan	*The DaVinci Code* (2003) Corgi Books
	Angels & Demons (2003) Corgi Books
Coelho, Paul	*The Alchemist* (2002) Harper Collins
Copper, Diana	*Little Light on Spiritual Laws* (2000) Hodder and Stoughton
	Transform Your Life (1993) Piatkus Books Ltd.
Edwards, Gill	*Living Magically* (1991) Piatkus Books Ltd.
Hay, Louise L.	*You Can Heal Your Life* (1984) Hay House Inc.
Linn, Denise	*Sacred Space* (2005) Rider and Co. (new edition)
McLean, Shirley	*Out on a Limb* (1983 Bantam Books
Redfield, James	*Celestine Prophecy* (1994) Bantam Books Transworld Publishers, a division of Random House Group
Weiss, Brian	*Only Love is Real* (1997) Piatkus Books Ltd.
	Through Time into Healing (2001) Piatkus Books Ltd.
	Many Lives, Many Masters (1988) Piatkus Books Ltd.

Workshops, Classes, Talks and Retreats, contact:
Marie at www.theenergywithin.co.uk or email mariec606@hotmail.com